Life in
Hong Kong

Titles in The Way People Live series include:

Cowboys in the Old West
Games of Ancient Rome
Life Among the Great Plains Indians
Life Among the Ibo Women of Nigeria
Life Among the Indian Fighters
Life Among the Pirates
Life Among the Puritans
Life Among the Samurai
Life Among the Vikings
Life During the Black Death
Life During the Crusades
Life During the French Revolution
Life During the Gold Rush
Life During the Great Depression
Life During the Middle Ages
Life During the Renaissance
Life During the Russian Revolution
Life During the Spanish Inquisition
Life in a Japanese American Internment
  Camp
Life in America During the 1960s
Life in a Medieval Castle
Life in a Medieval Monastery
Life in an Amish Community
Life in a Nazi Concentration Camp
Life in Ancient Athens
Life in Ancient China
Life in Ancient Egypt
Life in Ancient Greece
Life in Ancient Rome

Life in a Wild West Show
Life in Berlin
Life in Charles Dickens's England
Life in Communist Russia
Life in Genghis Khan's Mongolia
Life in Moscow
Life in the Amazon Rain Forest
Life in the American Colonies
Life in the Elizabethan Theater
Life in the Hitler Youth
Life in the North During the Civil War
Life in the South During the Civil War
Life in the Warsaw Ghetto
Life in Tokyo
Life in War-Torn Bosnia
Life of a Medieval Knight
Life of a Nazi Soldier
Life of a Roman Slave
Life of a Roman Soldier
Life of a Slave on a Southern Plantation
Life on Alcatraz
Life on a Medieval Pilgrimage
Life on an African Slave Ship
Life on an Everest Expedition
Life on Ellis Island
Life on the American Frontier
Life on the Oregon Trail
Life on the Pony Express
Life on the Underground Railroad
Life Under the Jim Crow Laws

THE WAY
PEOPLE
LIVE

Life in
Hong Kong

by Tony Zurlo

Lucent Books, 10911 Technology Place, San Diego, CA 92127

Library of Congress Cataloging-in-Publication Data

Zurlo, Tony.
  Life in Hong Kong / by Tony Zurlo.
      p. cm. — (The way people live)
Includes bibliographical references and index.
  ISBN 1-56006-384-X
  1. Hong Kong (China)—Juvenile literature.
I. Title. II. Series.
  DS796.H74 .Z87 2002
  951.25—dc21

                                                                2001002781

Contents

Discovering the Humanity in Us All

Books in The Way People Live series focus on groups of people in a wide variety of circumstances, settings, and time periods. Some books focus on different cultural groups, others, on people in a particular historical time period, while others cover people involved in a specific event. Each book emphasizes the daily routines, personal and historical struggles, and achievements of people from all walks of life.

To really understand any culture, it is necessary to strip the mind of the common notions we hold about groups of people. These stereotypes are the archenemies of learning. It does not even matter whether the stereotypes are positive or negative; they are confining and tight. Removing them is a challenge that's not easily met, as anyone who has ever tried it will admit. Ideas that do not fit into the templates we create are unwelcome visitors—ones we would prefer remain quietly in a corner or forgotten room.

The cowboy of the Old West is a good example of such confining roles. The cowboy was courageous, yet soft-spoken. His time (it is always a he, in our template) was spent alternatively saving a rancher's daughter from certain death on a runaway stagecoach, or shooting it out with rustlers. At times, of course, he was likely to get a little crazy in town after a trail drive, but for the most part, he was the epitome of inner strength. It is disconcerting to find out that the cowboy is human, even a bit childish. Can it really be true that cowboys would line up to help the cook on the trail drive grind coffee, just hoping he would give them a little stick of peppermint candy that came with the coffee shipment? The idea of tough cowboys vying with one another to help "Coosie" (as they called their cooks) for a bit of candy seems silly and out of place.

So is the vision of Eskimos playing video games and watching MTV, living in prefab housing in the Arctic. It just does not fit with what "Eskimo" means. We are far more comfortable with snow igloos and whale blubber, harpoons and kayaks.

Although the cultures dealt with in Lucent's The Way People Live series are often historically and socially well known, the emphasis is on the personal aspects of life. Groups of people, while unquestionably affected by their politics and their governmental structures, are more than those institutions. How do people in a particular time and place educate their children? What do they eat? And how do they build their houses? What kinds of work do they do? What kinds of games do they enjoy? The answers to these questions bring these cultures to life. People's lives are revealed in the particulars and only by knowing the particulars can we understand these cultures' will to survive and their moments of weakness and greatness.

This is not to say that understanding politics does not help to understand a culture. There is no question that the Warsaw ghetto, for example, was a culture that was brought about by the politics and social ideas of Adolf

Hitler and the Third Reich. But the Jews who were crowded together in the ghetto cannot be understood by the Reich's politics. Their life was a day-to-day battle for existence, and the creativity and methods they used to prolong their lives is a vital story of human perseverance that would be denied by focusing only on the institutions of Hitler's Germany. Knowing that children as young as five or six outwitted Nazi guards on a daily basis, that Jewish policemen helped the Germans control the ghetto, that children attended secret schools in the ghetto and even earned diplomas—these are the things that reveal the fabric of life, that can inspire, intrigue, and amaze.

Books in The Way People Live series allow both the casual reader and the student to see humans as victims, heroes, and onlookers. And although humans act in ways that can fill us with feelings of sorrow and revulsion, it is important to remember that "hero," "predator," and "victim" are dangerous terms. Heaping undue pity or praise on people reduces them to objects, and strips them of their humanity.

Seeing the Jews of Warsaw only as victims is to deny their humanity. Seeing them only as they appear in surviving photos, staring at the camera with infinite sadness, is limiting, both to them and to those who want to understand them. To an object of pity, the only appropriate response becomes "Those poor creatures!" and that reduces both the quality of their struggle and the depth of their despair. No one is served by such two-dimensional views of people and their cultures.

With this in mind, The Way People Live series strives to flesh out the traditional, two-dimensional views of people in various cultures and historical circumstances. Using a wide variety of primary quotations—the words not only of the politicians and government leaders, but of the real people whose lives are being examined—each book in the series attempts to show an honest and complete picture of a culture removed from our own by time or space.

By examining cultures in this way, the reader will notice not only the glaring differences from his or her own culture, but also will be struck by the similarities. For indeed, people share common needs—warmth, good company, stability, and affirmation from others. Ultimately, seeing how people really live, or have lived, can only enrich our understanding of ourselves.

A Successful Mix of Eastern and Western Cultures

When the United Nations analyzed 174 countries (including Hong Kong) in 2000 to assess their "quality of life," three of the four "Little Dragons" of Asia (Hong Kong, South Korea, Singapore, and Taiwan) ranked in the top 15 percent. Hong Kong placed ahead of South Korea and just behind Singapore (Taiwan was not listed). This favorable rating might surprise many people who see Hong Kong as an overcrowded, polluted city with no space to expand. But the UN's statistics show that Hong Kong is doing a good job of meeting the needs of its residents. According to the report, the city provides its "citizens [the ability] to lead a long and healthy life; to acquire knowledge; and to have access to a decent standard of living."[1]

Life in Hong Kong

Whenever people talk about life in Hong Kong, two major characteristics stand out: endless con-

Fast-Paced Living

Hong Kong leaves vivid memories with everyone who visits. In "Hong Kong: Citizens in a Bamboo Cage," travel specialist Lee Foster recalls his memories of the city, which reflect the busy pace of life in modern Hong Kong.

"Hong Kong remains in memory as a truck loaded with white ducks going to market, as a perpetual construction site where all the scaffolding is done in bamboo (the better to sway with the typhoon winds), and as the capital of high-stress business living. You won't find wide boulevards for the leisurely citizen or a grand design in urban planning, but you will find vitality. Even the Chinese language is an aggressive semi-shout, as if saying 'let's get on with it,' whatever we're doing. The friendlier the conversants, the higher the decibel level.

Hong Kong is cellular phones for the business person, who can now work even while commuting or sitting in restaurants. Helicopters hover over the water with tycoons who can't waste the time it takes a limo to get from the airport to their deal-making meeting in Central. Hong Kong is businessmen in suits sneaking a tai chi exercise motion or two, overhead walkways so people don't interfere with the flow of traffic. Hong Kong offers a human encounter that is brusque rather than friendly, the relationship you expect of the honest merchant rather than the personal friend. Hong Kong wears wealth proudly, whether it's the all-gold fillings in the mouth of a Hakka fisherwoman, the designer-jacket teenager with his compact disk Walkman, or the marbled office building. There is a slight element of British formality in this well-dressed world, coat and tie for the gentleman."

Hong Kong is a noisy, crowded city, famous for its many high-rises and hectic pace of life.

struction and the noisy, hectic pace of life. To those who regularly return to the city for business or family visits, old buildings have disappeared and newer, higher ones are replacing them. The construction contributes to the noise, becoming just one part of the symphony of sounds that characterize daily life in Hong Kong. Longtime Hong Kong observer Jan Morris recorded her impressions of the city:

> As time passes the noise increases. The schoolboys break into an argument. The small girls play merry games with chopsticks. The women talk very loudly with their mouths full. Outside the door [of the café where she is sitting] an electric drill starts up, and the café owner reaches over my head to turn up the volume of the TV. It doesn't matter in the least. . . . The now deafening variety of affairs in the café is a true microcosm of the Chinese city outside. The frank untidiness of the establishment, its free and easy way, the feeling that it has not been there very

long anyway, and may well have moved somewhere else next time I pass this way, is Chinese Hong Kong all over.[2]

Most Crowded City in the World

Hong Kong is made up of four major land areas: Hong Kong Island, Kowloon Peninsula, the New Territories, and the outer islands. With 1.5 million residents living on fifty square miles of land, Hong Kong Island has a population density of about thirty thousand persons per square mile. And most of them live on the northern half of the island. Hong Kong's business and banking district, located on the northwest side of Hong Kong Island in an area called Central, has the largest concentration of workers in the world.

Just across the harbor from Central is Kowloon Peninsula, which is home to some of the world's most crowded neighborhoods. The Kowloon district known as Mong Kok, with more

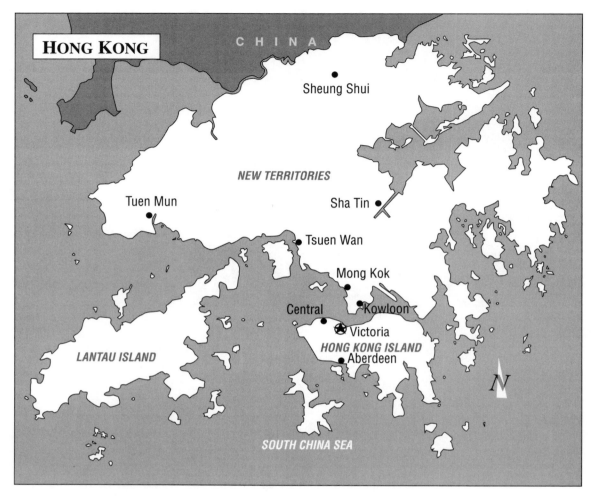

than 250,000 people per square mile, is said to be the most crowded area in the world. The New Territories, however, have grown into the largest area of Hong Kong. The town of Sha Tin, in the southeastern part, had about thirty thousand people in the early 1970s. Since that time, it has become a bustling city of 700,000 people.

East and West Meet

One reason Hong Kong has been able to grow so rapidly is the people's ability to blend Chinese traditions with Western ideas of business. Hong Kong has the second largest stock market in Asia, is one of the four major world traders in gold, and is the tenth largest banking center in the world. Yet, as author Peter Lok explains, "in an ultra-modern skyscraper [in Hong Kong], you might find a . . . religious shrine in a corner to a protective god. People are superstitious, yet use the latest computers and high-tech gadgets to full effect. Traditions die hard here and it is an exciting blend of old and new that makes sense to the locals, but is an enigma to outsiders."[3]

Getting Around

A tiny, crowded city, Hong Kong has only about 1,160 miles of highways. However, the city boasts about 450 vehicles for every mile of road, an extremely high density. Many of these are commercial vehicles, trucks, buses, and taxis. Some are private vehicles, although there are only about 350,000 privately owned automobiles registered in the city, meaning the vast majority of Hong Kong's residents do not own a car. If they did, the city would come to a standstill from the added congestion on the streets. For this reason, 90 percent of Hong Kong's 7 million people use public transportation to move around the city. This system, rated by *Asiaweek* magazine as among the best public transportation systems in the world, makes more than 10.5 million passenger trips each day.

Buses

Buses are the most commonly used form of public transportation, accounting for 52 percent of the passenger trips. The government has granted several private companies permission to operate bus routes throughout Hong Kong. The three major companies are the Kowloon Motor Bus Company (KMB), the New World First Bus Services (NWFB), and City Bus (CTB). KMB, the largest bus company in the city, serves Kowloon, the New Territories, and the cross-harbor tunnels to Hong Kong Island. With more than four thousand buses, about two-thirds of which are air-conditioned, the KMB carries about 3 million passengers a day, more than 1 billion passengers

a year, making it the largest public transport carrier in Hong Kong. KMB's buses are high-tech, efficient, and cheap, ranging from about 25 cents to about $3 (in U.S. money) per trip.

Hong Kong Island itself is served by two separate companies: the NWFB, with about 950 buses, and CTB, with about 850 buses. Both companies also make cross-harbor connections with KMB. CTB has a separate contract to connect to Hong Kong's Chek Lap Kok

Buses are the most common mode of transportation on Hong Kong's busy streets.

Hong Kong's roads are extremely crowded. In his website journal titled "Daily Life," Father Charlie Dittmeier, who taught for many years at Caritas Magdalene School in Hong Kong, describes trying to walk across one of Hong Kong's major intersections in November 1999: "I had to cross in front of a car inching out across the sidewalk into the street from a construction site. Cars reign supreme here, and from the driver's perspective I had darn well better not be in front of his car when he decides the approaching gap in traffic [is] long enough to allow him to squeeze in."

Airport on Lantau Island. Several smaller companies have government permission to run routes to other growing areas of Hong Kong. For example, the New Lantau Bus Company (NLB) serves Lantau Island with more than eighty buses, and the Long Win Bus Company (LW) covers North Lantau and the airport.

Another form of bus transportation is the public light bus (PLB). Numbering more than forty-three hundred, these small, sixteen-passenger buses, sometimes called maxicabs or minibuses, carry more than 1.5 million passengers to their destinations each day. Hong Kong's government has divided the PLBs into two categories: one group of buses are painted red, while the other group is green. The twenty-three hundred green buses are strictly regulated by the city's Transportation Department and follow preset routes, timetables, and charges. Passengers pay when they board. The government allows operators of the two thousand red PLBs, on the other hand, to set their own schedules and fares, so passengers pay according to the distance they travel.

Clean, Fast, and Efficient Trains

Trains and subways are the second most popular method of public transportation. Every day, 3.5 million people use Hong Kong's subways and trains. This accounts for 30 percent of the total passenger trips for all forms of public transportation. The Mass Transit Railway (MTR), for example, carries 2.4 million passengers between Kowloon and Hong Kong Island daily. For $1.60 (US) or less, passengers get a clean, fast, and efficient subway ride to almost anywhere in Hong Kong.

The city's other railway, the Kowloon-Canton Railway (KCR), was established in 1982. A year later the company electrified its system and added double tracks. The KCR was the first line to carry passengers from Kowloon into China before the 1997 handover of Hong Kong from the British to the Chinese, and by 2000, it was carrying more than 1 million passengers daily.

The negative side of riding any of these trains is the crowds. Buying tickets can be a wrestling match, as people elbow and push each other toward the ticket counter. Subway cars and stations are nearly always packed with people. And as soon as a train stops, people scramble and shove to get on to the cars. According to writer Randall van der Woning,

No matter whether you take the KCR or the MTR, people sprint to catch the train. Not stroll or walk, they run! Never mind if they are loaded down with shopping bags or briefcases. . . . The sprinters will queue [line up] at the edge of the platform, and when the train comes to a stop, they try to jam in to the car while the people inside are trying to get out.[4]

Trams

Buses and trains are two ways to get around the city, but in the northern section of Hong Kong Island, tourists and local residents who are not in a hurry often ride trams, or streetcars. The most popular tram has been in operation for a century. Operated by Hong Kong Tramways, it runs east-west parallel to Hong Kong Harbor. More than 280,000 people a day ride these streetcars for about 25 cents per trip for adults and half that for children.

A special tram on Hong Kong Island called the Peak Tram is operated by the Peak Tramways Company. Since 1888, this tram, which carries nine thousand workers and sightseers daily, has been carrying people from Central, the business hub of Hong Kong, up the 1,805-foot-high Victoria Peak. Known simply as the Peak, this attraction is one of the most popular recreational spots in Hong Kong because of the spectacular

The Peak Tram carries nine thousand passengers daily up the 1,805-foot-high Victoria Peak, where visitors enjoy a stunning view of surrounding areas.

view from the top. Besides the business district and harbor below, on clear days visitors can see northward past Kowloon and the mountainous New Territories and into mainland China.

Taxis

Taxis are the third most commonly used form of transportation in Hong Kong. Also regulated by the government, the approximately eighteen thousand registered taxis carry an estimated 1.3 million passengers daily. Taxis are divided into two types: urban and NT (New Territories), each differentiated by color. Another fifty or so taxis are licensed to operate exclusively on Lantau Island.

Of the two major types of taxicabs, the vast majority, more than fifteen thousand, are red with silver tops, designating them as urban taxis. These are authorized to travel only within Hong Kong Island and Kowloon and carry about 1.1 million people a day. About three thousand other taxis are green with white tops, though, and these are permitted to serve the New Territories; they carry about 208,000 passengers daily. Fares start at around $1.80 (US) and increase about 15 cents for each additional tenth of a mile.

Private Automobiles

Traveling around Hong Kong can be complicated and dangerous for even the most experienced drivers. Of a trip through the hills near where he worked, Charlie Dittmeier says, "I was traveling . . . on one of the large double-decker buses that often have to slow down or wait for oncoming traffic because the vehicles cannot pass side-by-side on the narrow, twisting lanes. . . . Our bus, swerving toward the curb to maneuver past an oncoming bus on a tight turn, brushed the rocky face of the cliff and a protruding rock smashed two of the bus's windows. No one was hurt but it's a wonder that doesn't happen more often."[5]

Besides the hilly terrain, drivers of private automobiles have to compete for parking spaces. Finding one can be quite a challenge and expense. The city government operates more than thirteen thousand on-street metered parking spaces that cost around HK$2 (approximately 13 US cents) for thirty minutes. The government also owns thirteen multistory parking garages with approximately seventy-five hundred spaces. The cost for parking in the garages varies depending on the location and time of use. In concentrated business areas, such as Kowloon Peninsula and Central on Hong Kong Island, drivers pay more

Rolls-Royce Capital

Only a small percentage of Hong Kong's residents own automobiles. However, the city's extremely wealthy residents can afford the best-made and most prestigious cars in the world. Their ownership of Mercedes Benzes, for example, is the highest of any nation per person outside of Germany. In addition, as the Hong Kong Tourist Association explains in the Internet article "Tops for Transit,"

"Hong Kong boasts the world's highest per capita ownership of Rolls-Royce cars, being home to about 1,500 (or 1%) of the car-maker's all-time production. In September 1991, the car-maker chose Hong Kong as the venue for the world's longest parade of Rolls-Royces up to that time, creating a Guiness world record for marshalling 104 cars for a charity fund-raising procession."

Taxis are a popular transportation option since few people own cars in Hong Kong.

than HK$20 an hour (about US$2.55) between 7 A.M. and 11 P.M. to park their cars at government-sponsored parking garages. The vast majority of parking spaces are privately owned and operated, however. Parking is outrageously expensive in these. In fact, one writer reports reading of a "parking space that sold for US$80,000."[6]

Making huge profits from selling parking spaces is common in Hong Kong. Although the number of private vehicles remains low, as the lifestyle and incomes of the city's residents rise, more people buy cars, and the demand for parking spaces increases. The number of spaces available, though, remains about the same. Thus, the people who own the parking spaces can make huge profits by selling them to wealthy businessmen. Dittmeier reported

that in 1998, "420 spaces were sold . . . [at] the average price per space . . . [of] $57,000. That's US dollars, not HK dollars. . . . 50 [of these spaces] were bought by one man for US$8.8 million!"[7]

Air Pollution

As a result of the high concentration of vehicles, especially the diesel-using taxis and buses, Hong Kong's air quality has deteriorated as rapidly as its economy has expanded. Vehicle exhausts are trapped by the mountainous and hilly terrain, especially in the late winter months. Thomas Chow, deputy secretary of Hong Kong's Environment and Food

Bureau, says, "We are very cramped and pollutants can't be dispersed easily."[8]

Such high levels of pollution—sometimes it is so bad it becomes difficult to see across Hong Kong Harbor, a distance of about one mile—lead to problems. The dirty air has blackened many of the concrete and brick-building walls, and Hong Kong authorities are concerned for the health of the city's inhabitants. Plato Yip, head of the environmental group Friends of the Earth, says that every year there are about 400,000 asthma cases attributed to the polluted air. And according to a recent report by former legislator Christine Loh's Citizens Party,

> Some 2,000 people a year die prematurely due to air pollution. The number of hospitalisation days for respiratory cases has also increased by 23% since 1996, a portion of which are almost certainly attributable to air pollution. Daily hospital admissions and daily mortality are adversely influenced by increases in NO_2 [nitrogen dioxide], SO_2 [sulfur dioxide], RSP [respirable suspended particles caused mostly by diesel-using vehicles] and ozone.[9]

Hong Kong authorities are seeking ways to solve the problem. One effort, closing parts of the commercial area in Central to vehicles, will bring some improvement. Another measure passed by Hong Kong's government increases the fines for driving vehicles that are heavy polluters, although the increase is small. Solving the problem in the near future, however, remains a difficult task because of the predicted growth of automobile ownership and its accompanying increase in traffic.

Ferries

One way to reduce air pollution is to use non-polluting forms of transportation. One form—ferries—is growing in popularity. People who cross Hong Kong Harbor to work or shop often take ferries. The Star Ferry Company operates two services directly from the Kowloon Peninsula to Central on Hong Kong Island. The Star Ferry carries more than eighty-one thousand passengers daily on the ten-minute trip across the harbor, and the fees are minimal, less than 35 cents (US). Author Jan Morris describes a typical ride:

> Chinese sailors in blue cotton uniforms deftly handle the ropes. . . . [The] iron . . . gate is lifted to allow [passengers] to board. . . . There are two classes, first on the upper deck, second below, but people of means [first class] often prefer to travel second class because they can get off the boat quicker when it docks. . . . [The boats are all] green-and-white boats of thirty-nine tons, traveling at an average speed of twelve knots and all named for stars—Long Star, Morning Star, Meridian, Celestial, Northern, Shining, Day, Silver and Twinkling Stars. They and their predecessors have been making the trip since 1868. [10]

Passengers on these boats are from every class and age group. Chinese students dressed in their school blazers carry satchels and tennis rackets. Housemaids crowd together gossiping, while businessmen dressed in conservative, striped dark suits fix their eyes on the skyscrapers across the harbor. Rebellious-looking, long-haired boys sneak looks at passengers, as young women dressed neatly in casual clothes and sneakers watch the harbor traffic.

In addition to the Star Ferry, there are fourteen *kaitos*, or private ferry services, licensed by the government to take people to locations other than Central and Kowloon Peninsula. One is the New World First Ferry Services, which carries passengers to and from the outlying islands. Another is the Discovery Bay Transportation Services, which takes passengers to and from the airport. Altogether, the various ferry services carry more than 57 million passengers a year.

Airways

Besides having one of the most efficient public transportation systems in the world, Hong Kong also has one of the world's most modern airports. This was not always the case. Until 1997, everyone flying into Hong Kong's airport had to endure one of the most dangerous approaches and landings in the world. Morris de-

scribes that approach at night: "The harbor unfolds itself around . . . [the plane's] windows, as the myriad [many varied] lights glitter, as first the mountains, then the skyscrapers rush by, and . . . [the plane] lands mysteriously on the runway among the waters, the deep dark blue of the seas on either side, the starry blue of the sky above, as in the middle of some fabulously illuminated bowl of glass."[11]

Many pilots dreaded the approach over Hong Kong Harbor, an approach requiring them to land on an old runway that protruded eight thousand feet into the harbor. In fact, landing in Hong Kong used to be so difficult that countries around the world used simulations of that runway to train pilots. Phil Parker,

Star Ferries transport more than 80,000 passengers across Hong Kong Harbor daily.

Chek Lap Kok Airport, which opened in 1998, is an ultramodern, super-efficient airport that accommodates 90,000 passengers daily.

an air traffic controller at the airport, writes that the "famous curved approach to Runway 13, close to the buildings and surrounding hills of the Kowloon Peninsula, is in aircraft simulators, both military and civil with every major operator in the world."[12] Furthermore, ship captains entering the harbor from the east had to be in constant contact with the airport towers so they would not interrupt landings and takeoffs.

Everything changed in 1998 with the opening of Chek Lap Kok Airport on Lantau Island,

which is many miles west of Hong Kong Island and Kowloon Peninsula. To build this ultramodern airport, construction crews leveled surrounding hills and filled uneven ground with dirt and rock. A massive highway system and a new train line were built to connect the airport to Kowloon and Hong Kong Island through tunnels; at 4,518 feet long, it is the world's longest road and rail suspension bridge.

In 2000, *Asiaweek* magazine named Chek Lap Kok Airport the best airport in Asia. Correspondent Maria Cheng writes, "Chek Lap

Kok is a futuristic vision, featuring open-concept halls that maximize the use of natural light. But looks aren't everything. Beneath its striking design, Chek Lap Kok is a model of efficiency that seamlessly transports some 90,000 passengers to and from Hong Kong every day."[13]

The new airport is just one aspect of Hong Kong's highly efficient transportation system, a system that has evolved in response to the city's dense population. Solving the problems of moving large numbers of people through Hong Kong and reducing the pollution that is an inevitable result have been challenges for the government, but most experts and city residents contend that they are, largely, succeeding.

City Life

The 7 million residents of Hong Kong have adapted comfortably to a grand medley of sounds and activities. The Cantonese dialect of Chinese, spoken by the majority of people in Hong Kong, requires eight different levels of sounds just to differentiate meanings of words. So in conversations, when the Chinese seem to be shouting at each other, they are actually just altering the intensity of the sounds to communicate effectively.

The sounds of Hong Kong extend beyond the unique language, however. Jan Morris describes a night along the waterfront of Hong Kong Harbor:

> The air is likely to be rich and humid, the sky is lit with the brooding glow of a great city's lights, blotting out the stars. It does not matter where I am, Kowloon or Hong Kong–side; around me always, beyond the little pool of quiet I have made for myself . . . the huge endless stir of the place, the roar of traffic, the passing of the ships, the comings and goings of the ferries, combine into one gigantic sensation of communal energy. . . .
>
> Among the mingled noises of the evening, one [sound] is generally inescapable, *thump, thump, thump,* somewhere or other along the waterfront, across the harbor, behind me in the recesses of the city or far away in the dark countryside beyond. It is the sound of a jackhammer, the leitmotif [key theme] of Hong Kong. [14]

The city's many jackhammers are likely to be clearing an area for the construction of another high-rise building. Because Hong Kong has very little land, the city has to expand upward, rather than horizontally. Senior editor of *Beijing Review* Wayan Vota calls this "vertical living." He writes, "four apartments will be joined together by a common elevator and stairs, then stacked one on top of the next, to dizzying heights." [15]

Teeming Masses

Very few people who work in Hong Kong live outside this high-energy, urban sprawl. In fact, 80 percent of the city's population lives on only 8 percent of the city's land. These people live mostly in flats, small apartments usually no larger than two small rooms. Often, the bottom floors of buildings are occupied by businesses. But above the store signs, buildings take on a second life—as the backdrop for residents' daily living. Residents store their belongings on balconies. Clothes hang from lines crisscrossing back alleys. Morris describes a typical street scene that appears throughout Hong Kong:

> the garish merry signs, the clamorous shopfronts, . . . the banners, the rows of shiny hanging ducks, the washing on its poles, the wavering bicycles, the potted plants massed on balconies, . . . the smells of cooking, spice, incense, oil, the racket of radio music and amplified voices, the half-

shouted conversation that is peculiar to Chinese meeting one another in the street, the ceaseless clatter of spoons, . . . coins, hammers and electric drills. [16]

The "hub" of all this activity is in the Central district on the north shore of Hong Kong Island. Packed with the hundreds of thousands of people who come in from other parts of Hong Kong during the day to work and the tens of thousands of entertainment seekers at night, Hong Kong Island is always crowded.

Three-Snake Soup

Along the shore a few blocks west of the skyscrapers in Central is a section of Hong Kong Island called Western, which retains much of the city's traditional Chinese lifestyle. Crowded at all times of day and night, Western contains many open-front shops, some of which display live snakes such as cobras and pythons in cages. Despite the obvious dangers of such animals, the Chinese believe that snake is a good food to eat in cold weather; the meat warms the body.

A cluttered, crowded street in Hong Kong's Central district, the "hub" of the city.

In fact, one of the city's most popular dishes is three-snake soup.

Other soups are popular too, though many seem odd to tourists. One soup in particular, birds' nest soup, is made from swallow nests imported from Thailand and Indonesia. In addition to the soup being a delicacy, author Lee Foster explains that the Chinese believe "Birds' nest soup make[s] women more beautiful."[17]

Kowloon

Just across the harbor from Central district lies Kowloon, a small area of twenty-nine square miles that is home to almost 2.5 million people. The popular waterfront walkway winds along the shoreline offering views of the Peak, the skyscrapers on Hong Kong Island, and the pink Hong Kong Cultural Center, opened in 1989 by Princess Diana and Prince Charles. The sounds of ships and boats drift up from the harbor. On almost any day, this waterfront is the site of a great variety of activities. One observer describes the scene:

Along the water we spotted numerous people fishing with a simple rod and string, sometimes alone, sometimes as a family. A large wedding party crowded around a plaza as professional photographers captured the happy bride and groom, with the Hong Kong cityscape as their backdrop. Two old men play a game of backgammon

Chinese Delicacies

Some of the foods that Hong Kong residents enjoy are not common in other parts of the world. One of these is birds' nest soup. On his website, Andy Carvin describes a wholesale goods market where restaurants find ingredients for some of their unique specialties, including birds' nest soup.

"We entered Sheung Wan [along the harbor on Hong Kong Island] along Des Voeux Road before cutting left on Sutherland Street. There were no particular landmarks that announced our entry into the district apart from the conspicuous appearance of signs with drawings of sharks and birds' nests. Over the decades, this particular strip of Sheung Wan had grown into a wholesale goods market for restaurants. Herbs and roots of all shapes and sizes could be found in the many shops along these roads. But there are two real reasons why restauranteurs bring big money when they come to this neighborhood, and both of them are soup. Bird nest soup and shark fin soup are sophisticated delicacies in Hong Kong, and diners pay top dollar for the best soups they can get. Along the walls of the shops we could see giant dried shark fins, some as large as a meter in length. These yellowish, leathery strips would then be chopped up and used to make a broth. Similarly, in store windows we found fancy boxes of bird nests, most of which were small enough for you to fit two or three of them in the palm of your hand. Compared to the shark fins I found the notion of using nests in soup a little more difficult to grasp. Apparently each nest contained a bed of nettles collected by certain species of birds in southeast Asia. The birds secrete a glue-like liquid that they use to cement the nettles together. When heated in water, the secretions and the nettles impart a unique (and apparently highly cherished) flavor to the soup."

A man admires his prized bird outside a shop in Mong Kok's Bird Garden market.

inside a stone stairwell, both guzzling large bottles of lager [beer].[18]

Just a couple of miles north of the Kowloon shoreline is the Mong Kok district. Mong Kok means "busy point," and in this small section of the city are some of the busiest markets in the world. *Washington Post* journalist Keith Richburg describes it as "a noisy, congested hub of outdoor markets and small shops, glitzy new department stores and small street-side stalls."[19]

Shops on some streets in Mong Kok specialize in a single type of product. For example, shops along Sai Yeung Choi Street sell audio and video equipment. Tung Choi Street, better known as Ladies Street, is lined with shops and sidewalk vendors selling products for women; from midmorning to late evening, everything from women's clothing to cosmetics are sold at very low prices. Close by are Fa Yuen Street, with its large number of sporting good shops, and Yuen Po, the location of the Bird Garden. Along Yuen Po, shop owners buy and sell songbirds, from starlings and mynahs to parakeets and cockatiels. Every day, in a noisy gathering, hundreds of songbird owners meet to show off their prized birds from all over the world.

Mixing of Cultures

On these streets and others all across the city, modern and traditional cultures collide. Rock and rap music blare from radios. Painted and neon signs hang in endless rows from buildings. Several thousand automobiles and dozens of double-decked buses compete for space on the packed roads. Crowds seem to move in an urban, quick-footed dance to avoid collision.

However, nearby, perhaps on the same street, kite makers and fortune-tellers offer their products. Storefronts are decorated in gold and red, and street vendors crowd the sidewalks. Some, like Chow Loi-fung, sit outside with their thread and needles, working at treadle-operated sewing machines. Writer Keith Richburg describes Chow as representative of many Hong Kong residents. According to Richburg, "Hong Kong is a city of alleyways and byways, markets and street stalls; it is a noisy, crowded, congested place where people [the mainstream] ride in minibuses, not taxis or limousines."[20]

Markets

Daily, many of these mainstream residents stroll through the hundreds of markets scattered throughout the city. They meet with friends, buy products, or just look around. Two of the largest markets in Hong Kong are the indoor Central Market on Hong Kong Island and the outdoor Temple Street Market in Mong Kok.

Central Market opens early in the morning and closes by evening. Vendors on the fourth floor sell lingerie, jewelry, souvenirs, and fast food; the other floors house a fresh food market. Chinese customers often shop at Central Market early in the morning to buy their fresh foods from vendors at concrete stalls. Almost any food imaginable can be found there, including live crabs, prawns, eels, chicken's feet, sea cucumbers, lotus root, tongues, ears, and animal intestines. The meat at Central Market is fresh; butchers slaughter live animals here and prepare the meat and body parts for sale.

Temple Street Market, on the other hand, stays open late and becomes lively at night, when the majority of shoppers come looking for bargains. For several blocks, shops and outdoor vendors lay out items on tables beneath shop awnings. Hundreds of small restaurants compete with sidewalk cooks. Butchers in one shop sell the internal organs of animals, while a couple of stores away teenagers thumb through stacks of electronic computer games. People stroll beneath neon signs that cast a golden hue across the night market. Temple Street is a flea market, where shoppers might pause to watch a group of singers performing Chinese opera on the street. Others stop at one of the dozens of fortune-tellers offering their talents as palm and tarot card readers.

In 1999, visitor Jeff Booth reported his impressions of shopping in the Temple Street Market:

> We picked our way through narrow aisles lit by bare light bulbs swaying from makeshift power lines, their pale yellow light illuminating a museum of junk. Or treasures, depending on your tourist dollar. The vendors seemed arranged almost chronologically with respect to their wares. Starting at one end, piles of Qing dynasty opium pipes, imperial sunglasses (wire-rimmed John Lennon jobs), and small blue and white porcelain bowls the hawker [seller] swore were Ming dynasty. As we slowly moved down the street, the years fell away as fast as prices dropped, and soon we were haggling over colonial British jewelry boxes and faded . . . photographs of polo players. The next tables had stacks of [Communist revolutionary] Mao Zedong pins in every shade of red. The seeming contradiction didn't phase the seller; he knew people wanted to buy these

trinkets, and who cares about idealism when money could be made. Pure Hong Kong. A smattering of [Communist leader] Deng Xiaoping posters segued into monstrous piles of posters of Cantonese pop stars, pirated video DVDs, pornography, Tommy Hilfiger rip-offs, leather purses, remnant souvenirs of the '97 Handover, and the most ubiquitous symbol of Hong Kong today—cell phones.[21]

Booth's experience with cell phones at the Temple Street Market is true of most of Hong Kong. Throughout the city, cell phones ring continuously. Rich or poor, almost everyone in Hong Kong seems to own one. In fact, Hong Kong has the highest number of cell phones per person in the world. They ring constantly on the streets, in buildings, in movie houses, and in restaurants. Many of the captains of small boats in the harbor communicate by cell phone rather than radio. Even schoolchildren carry them as they shop after school for the latest popular CDs and eat a snack at McDonald's.

A night vendor prepares and displays a variety of delicacies at the outdoor Temple Street Market in Mong Kok.

Homeless Amid Affluence

Amid the ringing cell phones and money spent in markets, at least a half-million Hong Kong residents live below the poverty line. About two thousand of them are homeless. Some are crippled, like Chan Pok-wah, an amputee beggar who waits for handouts at a tunnel that connects the Star Ferry with one of Hong Kong's many expensive luxury hotels. Others, like Tang Chu-yuen, are refugees who fled communism in mainland China and worked for decades at odd jobs throughout Hong Kong.

Tang Chan and many others suffer health or legal problems that leave them with no money. And in an expensive city like Hong Kong, having no money means those city residents must rely on the few available government social programs and shelters. Today, says Keith Richburg in his *Washington Post* online article "Amid the Affluence, City's Homeless Are Nearly Invisible," Tang lives "on Shanghai Street, one of the oldest roads in the heart of congested Kowloon, in a densely populated neighborhood packed with market stalls, hardware shops, cramped 'cage house' apartments for the poor . . . and a homeless shelter in an old red brick government building."

A woman gives change to a homeless man in Hong Kong.

Calm in the Midst of Chaos

When they are not talking on their cell phones, Hong Kong's residents visit the city's many parks to relax, exercise, play tennis, read newspapers, picnic, and meet friends. Early every morning, thousands of elderly Chinese can be found in the parks stretching in the slow-motion exercise called tai chi.

Two parks stand out on Hong Kong Island as retreats from the hectic pace of life. One, Hong Kong Park, opened in 1991, is located a few blocks south of the harbor in the middle of the banking district. The park is small, about twenty acres, but it seems like a secluded sanctuary. Within its boundaries are small lakes, artificial waterfalls, a tai chi garden, a large rain-forest aviary, a modern conservatory, a greenhouse with more than two hundred kinds of tropical plants, and other attractions. Steep hills on one side of the park help preserve a sense of isolation.

Just a couple of miles east is another of Hong Kong Island's popular parks, Victoria Park. Its forty-two acres include special areas built for swimming, tennis, handball, soccer, basketball, roller-skating, jogging, and go-cart racing. Victoria Park also has several outdoor restaurants for diners. A very popular flower market is held in the park every year just before the Chinese New Year, and during the fall, city residents celebrate a lantern carnival in the park. During the carnival, colorfully lighted lanterns designed with calligraphy, classical scenes, and even modern rock idols hang from the trees.

Just a few blocks north of the Star Ferry terminal in Kowloon, Hong Kong residents find the thirty-three acre Kowloon Park a quiet retreat from the busy life around them. The park includes the city's Museum of History, a Chinese garden with lotus pond, a sculpture walk with works by Hong Kong artists, an aviary, a water garden, three roof gardens, an indoor Olympic-sized swimming pool, restaurants, and plenty of space to just sit and relax.

Hong Kong's government has also set aside large blocks of land in the New Territories for wildlife reserves. One of these, Mai Po Marshes in the far northeastern corner of the New Territories, has become a popular bird sanctuary. About four hundred different species of birds—from ducks and cormorants to the rare black-faced spoonbill and dalmatian pelican—have been recorded within Mai Po's 939 acres of mangrove forests and fish and shrimp ponds.

Amidst the towering skyscrapers of Hong Kong Island's bustling business district, residents can find nature and tranquility at Hong Kong Park.

Another large reserve is Kam Shan Country Park in the northwestern part of Kowloon. Besides the many kinds of birds that nest at Kam Shan, the park is especially popular for its large population of rhesus monkeys.

Rural Hong Kong

Although most residents of Hong Kong live in the city's urban areas, some live on the outlying islands. Rocky and very small, the islands are home to only a few thousand people, who live mostly by fishing and farming. Most of these islands defy Hong Kong's reputation as a modern metropolis. One, Cheung Chau, does not allow motorized vehicles. Many of Cheung Chau's nearly forty thousand inhabitants are fishermen who ply the ocean around Hong Kong and the waters hundreds of miles to the south. In recent years, however, because Cheung Chau is less than an hour from Hong Kong Island by ferry, the island has become home to hundreds of wealthy businessmen who want to live outside the chaos of urban Hong Kong.

Cheung Chau is also popular because of the eight-day Bun Festival, held there each year in late April or early May. The famous Pak Tai Temple (North God Temple) is the center of the celebration. Dating back to 1777, the festival features lion dances, international and local celebrities, and a parade with children dressed up in costumes representing personalities from traditional myths. Many of the costumed children on parade seem to glide along above the crowd. Art teacher David Clarke explains the secret to this popular illusion: "As part of the festival there are floats on which one child appears to hold up another in defiance of the laws of gravity. In this case the girl on top seems to be balancing on a teapot and various other vessels which in turn are balancing on a spear held by the boy below. In fact there is a metal structure (hidden inside the children's clothes, the teapot, and so on) which supports the upper child's weight." [22]

The main purpose of the Bun Festival is to gain the favor of Pak Tai, the god who rules the ocean and who can protect the people from spirits that return to the island during this time of year. To please Pak Tai, the islanders construct three 52-foot-high bamboo towers and cover them with thousands of cooked buns flavored with a paste made from lotus flower seeds. Supposedly, wandering spirits will then be satisfied with something to eat and return to their spirit world. The small pastries are left out for three days, and then a group of men take them down and distribute them throughout the island.

Lantau Island

A second rural island is Lantau Island. Nearly three times as large as Hong Kong Island, Lantau Island has only thirty thousand people. The small number of residents preserves the natural scenery of rolling mountains and Buddhist monasteries for which Lantau is known. Po Lin, Precious Lotus Monastery, near the top of Lantau Peak, is the most popular monastery on the island. It is particularly famous for the outdoor bronze statue of Buddha. Rising 100 feet high and weighing 276 tons, Po Lin's seated Buddha is the world's largest outdoor seated Buddha.

The island's tranquil atmosphere is being threatened, however. With the opening of the Chek Lap Kok Airport, urban growth has begun to spread to Lantau Island. Highways and housing developments are beginning to sprout up near the northern and western coastline. By 2005, a Disney theme park will begin attracting millions of new visitors throughout the year, further upsetting the island's reputation as a peaceful retreat.

Visitors ascend the steps to the 100-foot-high Buddha at the popular Precious Lotus Monastery on Lantau Island.

Low Crime Rate

Whether on the islands or in the bustling downtown area, Hong Kong is one of the safest cities in the world. According to government statistics, crime has declined steadily over the past few years. In 1995, the number of overall violent crimes was 17,087; the figure had dropped to 14,812 in 2000, and only a few of these were homicides. In 1996, researchers found that Hong Kong had a rate of 1.23 homicides per 100,000 population, a tiny number when compared with New York's 16.1 and Chicago's 29.9. Hong Kong is also among the safer cities in terms of burglaries, with only 223 per 100,000 people. By contrast, the figure for Chicago was more than 1,000 per 100,000 people in 1999.

Some of this low crime rate can be attributed to the government's spending and emphasis on law enforcement. During the late 1990s, Hong Kong had the world's sixth highest number of police per population, 640 per 100,000. The government also maintains an auxiliary police force of around five thousand; those officers are on-call twenty-four hours a day to supplement the regular police. The two forces combined give Hong Kong one police officer for every 202 persons. To further discourage major crime, government agencies and businesses hire a high number of private security guards.

There are other reasons for the good safety record. For one, everyone over fifteen years of age must carry an identity card and must produce it when asked by a police officer. Furthermore, Chinese cultural values and strong family bonds have traditionally deterred criminals. Elsie Tu, founder of the Mu Kuang School for poor children in Hong Kong, says the tradition of family loyalty is a major factor in the low crime rate in Hong Kong. She writes, "The reason crime is low is that the family is strong."[23]

In their ability to keep crime rates down, as in every other aspect of city life, the residents of Hong Kong blend traditional and modern culture.

Family and Home Life

The residents of Hong Kong construct their families and home life around the teachings of a sixth-century B.C. philosopher named Confucius. Although some people in Hong Kong worry that the tight family values Confucianism encourages are loosening under the pressures of twenty-first-century life, most agree with writer Elsie Tu, who says, "Confucianism is very deep in the Chinese mind. The Chinese are still following the Confucian ideal, even if they cannot articulate the specifics of the philosophy."[24]

Confucianism

Confucius taught that good families were built on the principles of respect for each other and obedience of the young to their elders; a society would prosper as a result because each family would be a self-governing unit. If anyone in the family caused trouble in the community, shame would fall on the entire family. In this environment, the male family head was the sole authority, but fathers and husbands were expected to teach others proper behavior by living a compassionate and moral life.

This Confucian view of family still extends into all aspects of Hong Kong life. For example, there are tens of thousands of small, family-owned businesses in the city. They are usually run by the male family head, and family and kin are expected both to participate in and benefit from the business. Writer Elizabeth Chin says that in Hong Kong,

Younger family members are often brought into the firm [business] to safeguard family interests. There is also a strong element of trust for kinship, and for people who speak the same dialect, or have come from the same clan or village. This enables transactions to be done informally and swiftly. Many family-owned firms have become international corporations. Although these organizations are

The teachings of sixth-century B.C. philosopher Confucius have had a lasting effect on many aspects of Hong Kong life.

Traditional Gender Roles in the Home

Confucian teachings place the male at the head of the household. All final decisions on everything from business matters, to child raising, to purchases were subject to his approval. Women, on the other hand, had little (if any) say in family matters. Instead, they were expected to take care of the household and do all the domestic chores. Although this has changed in many homes, writer Michele Tang (in "Gender Inequality in Household") describes how traditional Confucian attitudes of male dominance still prevail in some Hong Kong families.

"Twenty-two-year-old Amy comes from a traditional . . . family, which is often known for its strict male dominance. She told of her unfair treatment in her family.

'In my family,' said Amy, 'male members do not need to do any housework. Female members are responsible for all the domestic chores.'

Her family may be one of the many patriarchal families in Hong Kong. While feminists raise their voices against evident inequalities in the workplace, gender inequalities also occur in the household, mostly in implicit forms.

The society assigns specific roles to its male and female members. As a result, men and women are expected to have different attitudes and behaviour.

In traditional Chinese families, females are assigned the role of housekeepers while males are regarded as breadwinners.

Prof. Maria Tam Siu Mi, associate professor of the Department of Anthropology of The Chinese University of Hong Kong, said due to the assignation of roles, 50 percent of women have to leave the labour force after their marriages. The phenomenon of gender inequality is hence reinforced.

'In families,' said Prof. Tam, 'women are not paid for doing housework because society perceives this as their responsibility and takes this for granted.

'Since women do not earn money to support the family, they have no authority to make decisions for the family. As a result, females are considered as less clever and competent than males.'

In Chinese culture, the social role that a female plays is determined by her relationship with males. This thinking also reinforces gender inequality.

'When a girl is young,' said Prof. Tam, 'she is treated as her father's daughter. When she is grown up, she is treated as her husband's wife.

'Society does not consider a female as an individual and so the idea of gender inequality is strengthened.'"

managed more in a western fashion, it is never at the cost of weakening family control in the business. [25]

Housing for the Well-Off

As in work, several generations of a Chinese family traditionally lived together on the same plot of land, or compound. In modern Hong Kong, however, there is too little land for the city's 7 million residents to live comfortably. This drives the price of land and construction out of the range of most people and makes it difficult for large families to live together. As a result, only the well-off can afford adequate housing in Hong Kong. In Fairview Park, a New Territory suburb of twenty thousand, for instance, residents live in two-story homes with tiny front and back yards and a car port. To afford these homes, families must at least be in the upper middle class. Usually, both the husband and wife work full-time. Their jobs will pay relatively well, more than $20,000 (US) each annually. The combined income of $40,000 (US) places them in the top 10 to 15 percent of Hong Kong households.

Other members of the city's upper class come from families who themselves have money. Regina Wong, a ninth-grade biology teacher at Maryknoll Convent School, is a good example of this. Her upper-middle-class background provided her with the opportunities to be successful. Wong's parents sent her to the United States for college. There she married an American who worked in the computer field. His company transferred him to Hong Kong, and today they live in a three-story home near Guangdong Province in the northern section of the New Territories. Every day she drives her BMW into crowded Kowloon to teach.

The city's very rich live even more extravagantly. They have villas on the outer islands for vacation and mansions in the hills of the New Territories or southern Hong Kong Island. Others buy three-thousand-square-foot apartments on the Peak for $2 to $3 million (US). Many of the multimillionaires live dozens of floors above the commotion of the city, and have views that look out over the harbor.

Victor Fung is one such resident. With his brother, Fung runs Li and Fung, a trading company started by his grandfather. Fung explains with pride that "In 1906 . . . we [his family] were the first to bypass the British hongs . . . [trading companies] and set up a real trading company in Hong Kong. . . . [Fung's grandfather knew English and] was able to communicate with buyers and sellers overseas. Our company traded rattan, porcelain. Now we're a $2 billion trading house—a lot of consumer products, garments, textiles, toys."[26]

When Victor Fung went in search of a home, he kept in mind his traditional Confu-cian values. Today, says one journalist, Fung is "A man both modern and traditional. Fung lives in a penthouse with a spectacular view of Hong Kong atop a 30-story building he owns that stands on the site of the first family home. His mother lives across the hall in the other penthouse. His brother lives downstairs."[27]

Housing for the Majority

Victor Fung is the exception. Owning a home for the vast majority of Hong Kong residents means a two-room flat that would be substandard in the United States. Writer Peter Lok describes the rows upon rows of "Newer apartment blocks . . . often 40 stories or higher, with 8 apartments [on each] floor. You get a weird display of old and new buildings abutting together. Quite strange seeing shiny new stainless steel against old pollution yellowed concrete."[28] In these crowded buildings, often three generations live together, holding on to their Confucian idea of family. To create some sense of privacy, they hang curtains or place wooden partitions to divide up the rooms.

From May through early October, Hong Kong is hot and sticky, with temperatures as high as the mid-nineties and humidity usually above 70 percent. During these long steamy months, residents open windows (and sometimes doors) to circulate the air. The rainy season in Hong Kong begins in March and lasts until October. During this period, the city can get up to sixty of its annual eighty-three inches of rain, some of it brought by typhoons. Such humidity attracts all kinds of bugs, and most of the year, residents must fight off mosquitoes and other pests. One city resident describes the inevitability of sharing life with these creatures:

Geckos are lizards that are part of life in Hong Kong. They are in most houses, usually on the ceiling or high up on the walls. Sometimes you catch a glimpse of one as it skitters across the wall. Or it just sits in place, waiting for an insect to come into range. Basically they are helpful because they eat a tremendous amount of insects, but they can often be a nuisance when they poop on any papers you leave uncovered on the desk overnight. They also have a bad habit, in my room, of chirping in the middle of the night from the bookcase and awakening me. [29]

Inside the Home

Furniture for a typical Hong Kong family is practical, rather than decorative, mainly be-

cause there is just not enough room. Young couples just starting their married life often live with very little furniture at all. One resident who attended a young couple's housewarming writes, "They [the couple] have fixed it up really nice and added some partial interior walls to divide up the 20'x20' creatively. . . . [We] guests take off our shoes and sit on large pillows on the floor. There isn't room for furniture except for a low table and a stand for the television. The flat is on the sixth floor, and we can look directly into the sixth-floor windows of a garment factory across the street." [30]

The apartments of the middle class are sometimes better furnished, but hardly much larger. The rooms are a mixture of old China and high-tech. On the one hand, the Chinese like to display photographs of family members

A typical Hong Kong apartment is tiny and sparsely furnished.

Hong Kong's lower classes often endure terrible living conditions in concrete tenement buildings; this slum housed 30,000 people before it was torn down in the early 1990s.

and often hang pictures of scenery and artistic calligraphy on the walls. On the other, children usually share one bedroom, and around the room they accumulate mementos of their lives. Movie and rock star pictures hang on the walls; boys' skateboards are stored under the bed, and girls' closets are stocked with trendy blue jeans and colorful t-shirts.

Because of the small space, families tend to have few if any unneeded items. Children's bedrooms usually have a single or double bed, a dresser, and a work area with a desk, chair, and a bookcase. Because the average apartment usually has only two rooms, the other room will have another bed where the parents sleep. During the day, that bedding is folded and put in one corner so the bed itself becomes a place to sit. This room will also usually have a small coffee table, a small couch, a fold-out table for dining, and some chairs.

Most middle-class families have their own small kitchen with a refrigerator and gas stove. Many also own an air conditioner for the hot summer months. Televisions, DVD players, radios, and a telephone are also among a home's common appliances. Increasingly, families have computers connected to the Internet. In fact, with more than 40 percent of the population online, Hong Kong ranks fourth highest in the world in homes connected to the Internet.

Homes of the Lower Class

In contrast, lower-income families generally share appliances, televisions, and even a stove and concrete shelving for utensils. These families usually live in high-rise, concrete tenement buildings. Each floor often has one kitchen area set aside for all the people of that floor to use to cook. In addition, families on the same floor often share a single bathroom.

The apartments themselves usually consist of only one room, often less than two hundred square feet, with concrete floors and walls. In that one room there might be an old bed, a table, and a few chairs.

Sometimes Hong Kong's lower classes live in terrible conditions. A group of students in Hong Kong led by Zainab Aziz participated in a journalism training project that investigated the living conditions of the poor. They went to Sham Shui Po, one of the more crowded districts of Kowloon. There, above a store selling the latest and most expensive types of electronic supplies sits what residents sarcastically call "the Penthouse." Aziz writes that as he and his fellow students reached the top of the stairs, they were "surrounded by a mess of concrete, wires and corrugated tin. The sunroof was a hole [in] . . . the roof that could be covered up with a slab of corrugated tin when it rained." Seven families were living in an area about fifty by fifty feet. One husband and wife had been living for twenty-five years in a fifteen-square-foot room. Another family of five, the Chuens, "lived in a room less than 100 [square] feet! . . . Mr. Chuen works as a night-shift security guard, and his wife works as a cleaner. His two elder daughters, aged 21 and 18, were graduated and his youngest son, aged 12, is a student. . . . [Mr. Chuen] pointed to the only furniture in the room—a bunk bed. 'Our whole family lives here. I and my wife sleep at the lower bunk, my kids at the upper bunk.'" The families had to share the cooking area and bathroom. And although the building had electricity, Aziz writes, "the number of open wires . . . made this place an enormous fire hazard. The kitchen and the toilets were in close proximity to one another and the water flowing out of the bathroom flowed into the kitchen where many of the utensils were left on the floor due to lack of space." [31]

Government Assistance

Housing issues were not always so dire in Hong Kong. In fact, space didn't really become a major problem until the 1950s when up to a million refugees fled Communist southern China for Hong Kong. At first the refugees lived in sprawling camps of huts made from scrap lumber and metal, cardboard boxes, tents, just about any material they could dredge up from the dumps. The government, alarmed over the hundreds of thousands of people living in such appalling conditions, began to construct concrete high-rise buildings with minimal conveniences. Refugees by the tens of thousands moved in. Usually dozens lived together in one- and two-room flats.

Today, the government continues to build thousands of new apartments in huge housing projects throughout the New Territories. These massive high-rise buildings usually include enough apartments for more than thirty thousand people. One development in Tuen Mun district in the New Territories has more than nine thousand units and houses more than thirty-five thousand people. New developments such as this also include schools, shopping malls, supermarkets, clubhouses, amphitheaters, parks, fountains, and other services.

In addition, the government operates two major housing programs. One helps people rent apartments in the city. In 2000, more than 2.2 million people, 32 percent of the population, lived in public rental housing, and another 114,500 were on the waiting list. On average, tenants who participate in the government's rental program pay about 35 percent of the total rent of their apartment. The government pays the rest.

The other program offered by the government provides assistance to residents who want to buy their apartments. Because of this government program, home ownership in Hong Kong has risen for several years, and at the end of 2000 it stood at 51.4 percent (out of about 2.4 million households). Depending on a family's income, the government offers a variety of loan packages, from no-interest loans to government subsidies.

Family Budgets

Besides the rent or mortgage, families must use their monthly income to pay for food, electricity, gas (most cooking is done with gas), transportation to work, school supplies, and uniforms. With the money they have left over, they try to save for recreational activities such as attending movies, going to amusement parks, and eating out at restaurants.

The average middle-class family in Hong Kong makes around HK$10,000 (about $1,250 US) a month. In many families, however, once the couple has children, only the husband works full-time, so most people are not even this well-off. In fact, the average working-class family brings in less than HK$4,500 (about $560 US) monthly. These families make sacrifices and cut corners. So, even though the family unit is strong and thriving in Hong Kong, family life can be stressful.

Hong Kong's government has built thousands of high-rise apartment buildings in the New Territories to accommodate the city's growing population.

Food Lovers

No matter what a family's budget, however, the people of Hong Kong are food lovers, and they try to eat well. In fact, the common greeting in Hong Kong is the centuries-old phrase *"Sek joh fan, meiya?"* (Have you eaten yet?) The answer is generally "yes," as the Chinese eat three set meals each day. Congee (rice porridge) and pastries usually make up the normal breakfast. For lunch and dinner, rice is usually combined with vegetables and meats such as fish, pork, or chicken. People also eat many different kinds of fruit, from oranges and watermelons to tropical fruits such as pineapples, mangoes, and papaya.

Recently, though, people in Hong Kong are finding it more and more difficult to take time out to cook. As a result, many people have tea and bread or other foods that can be prepared quickly for breakfast. Many children stop on their way to school to buy breakfast buns from street vendors, and some students eat lunch at fast food restaurants. Lunch for many workers is also a problem. With no time to return home for lunch, they stop at a fast food restaurant or buy something from a food vendor on the street such as a rice box, a prepackaged meal usually made up of fried rice and barbecued meat.

Despite their issues with time, most Hong Kong residents try to prepare the majority of their meals at home. Every day, women shop for fresh foods in markets and grocery stores. Researchers report that "The first [study used to track consumer purchases in 2000] revealed that a typical Hong Kong household makes over thirty shopping trips each month, visiting a wet market [market with independent vendors selling fresh food] 16 times and the supermarket 14 times. The average household spent roughly $98 (HK) [about $12.50 US] per shopping trip with 80% going to food and beverage of which 45% is spent on fresh foods."[32]

Two men enjoy a meal at a Hong Kong shop. The people of Hong Kong place a high value on eating well.

Although many women in Hong Kong work outside the home, they are still primarily responsible for cooking, housework, and child care.

Women's Lives

Traditional values still prevail in Hong Kong, so whether women work outside the home or not, they still do most of the shopping, cooking, and housework. However, slowly, young women are challenging this stereotype. A number of influences, from education to Western-influenced popular culture, are changing youths' attitudes toward women's roles in society. Today, women in Hong Kong own and run their own companies, become lawyers for multinational corporations, and are elected representatives to government and neighborhood organizations.

One result of these new roles is a change in the institution of marriage. First, women and men are marrying much later in life. In 1971, the average age of marriage for women was twenty-three, and for men it was twenty-nine. By 1999, the ages had risen to twenty-seven and thirty, respectively. Today, when women in Hong Kong finish their education, many go into the workforce and make money instead of marrying immediately. When they do marry, they often remain in the workforce, contributing to their family income. Furthermore, women are having fewer children. In Hong Kong, the number of children per 1,000 women between fifteen and forty-nine years of age has dropped from about 3.5 in 1971 to 1.3 in 1995.

These trends conflict sharply with the old Confucian values, but gender roles are still distinct in Hong Kong, even with the calls for change. In fact, one researcher concluded that "participation of women in the work force . . . [and] efforts by feminist movements" have failed to bring about "gender equality or an abolition of gender stereotypes in . . . daily life, the media, or society at large."[33] For this reason, there is a lot of pressure on women to conform. Many women stop working after marriage. Professor Maria Tam Siu Mi, associate professor at the Chinese University of Hong Kong, believes that as many as half of all working women quit their jobs once they marry. They become traditional wives who stay home to take care of the apartment, shop, and raise the children. Very few husbands get involved with the duties of cooking, cleaning, and child care.

Single Parenthood

Marriages in which women continue to work after having children run a higher risk of divorce than those in which women stay home. In fact, divorces in Hong Kong have increased rapidly since the mid-1990s. In one two-year period they rose by 50 percent, from 10,292 in 1995 to 15,037 in 1997. Although still low by many nations' standards, in Hong Kong's Confucian-guided society, divorce was rare before the 1990s.

The recent rise in divorce rates has also led to a rise in the number of single mothers in Hong Kong. These women find themselves trying to balance the role of breadwinner with that of caregiver. In doing so, many single mothers find they cannot continue to work full-time and quit their jobs. Others lose their jobs because they must dedicate more time to their children. In fact, a recent report indicates that nearly 40 percent of single mothers are without jobs.

Single mothers often have to turn to government assistance to get by. And many just barely survive. Thirty-seven-year-old Zeng Jihuan's tight budget is typical. She lives with her two children on about $1,028 (US) a month. After paying $523 for rent, she has to juggle the remaining $505 on food, utilities, and other expenses, including $2.50 each time she or her children have to visit the public hospital if one of them gets sick. She says, "I feel bad not being able to give more to my kids. They come home from school babbling [about] what others have, and what they don't have."[34]

Youth Issues

Zeng's children are typical of Hong Kong's youth. They want the same games and clothes that their peers have. Young people in Hong Kong are very much like their counterparts elsewhere. They follow the careers of their favorite rock singers and movie stars, they dress according to the latest fads, and they worry about their future. In their Confucian society, though, these young people, especially teenagers, seem rebellious, a generation with no direction or discipline. One observer says that children in Hong Kong are not as well behaved as they used to be: They "fight outside the school, smoke in toilets,

Some people blame Western influences for increasing rebellious behavior and liberal attitudes among Hong Kong teenagers.

make noise, litter, and be impertinent. . . . Not all girls behave as well as they did and I blame the spread of Western feminism."[35]

The youngsters themselves agree. Surveys show that the ideological gap between young people and their parents is getting larger. The most striking finding was in response to questions about unwed mothers. Recently a Hong Kong youth group found that 40 percent of the young people surveyed "accepted a woman's right to have a baby and form a family only with her child without marriage."[36] The respondents also expressed much more liberal attitudes than previous generations toward premarital sex and living together before marrying.

One major influence on the changing ideas of Hong Kong's youth is their daily exposure to music and videos that make rebellion against adult values attractive. Officials in Hong Kong are concerned that these rebellious attitudes have brought about an increase in youth crime in recent years. According to police records, drug offenders below twenty-one years of age increased 77.5 percent in 2000. And of the 2,490 youths in jail in June 2000, 520 were arrested for drug-related crimes.

By Western standards, however, Hong Kong's youth is well behaved. Young people in Hong Kong still rank having a strong family as their most valued goal. And in a recent survey, the vast majority (94 percent) of young people said they believed in obeying the law and that education was important (89 percent).

Such statistics show that Confucian values are still strong in Hong Kong. The tight family unity based on Confucianism has provided the city's people with the foundation for stability. And even as things change, as women become more independent and teenagers question the authority of their elders, the ancient beliefs remain important.

4 Education

In an effort to teach moral integrity and the idea that education is a means to success, schools in Hong Kong have traditionally stressed discipline. Strictly run classrooms, uniforms, and morning checks and assemblies are common. Teachers expect students to obey without question. To reinforce this discipline, students in both primary and secondary levels are required to wear uniforms. Usually, girls wear dark-colored skirts and light-colored blouses, with a tie and blazer or sweater. The boys wear similar colored pants and shirts with ties and blazers.

Students form in assemblies every morning in an orderly manner. Secondary school teacher Marcia Hohmann writes, "The whole process reminds me of a military-style line-up: orders are shouted, actions are performed swiftly, effi-ciently and—most importantly—quietly." Students must go to assigned places. And toward the end of the assembly comes Hohmann's "favorite part of the morning—uniform check: time to get up close and personal as I make my way through my class, checking for plain white socks, correct length trousers and skirts, short fingernails, neatly kept hair and neckties in place."[37] Parents, in general, believe these practices prepare children (specifically boys) for success.

The Function of Education

For two thousand years, the Chinese faith in education as a means to success never wavered. Confucian scholars over the centuries pro-

Students at Hong Kong schools are required to wear uniforms and are taught the importance of order and discipline.

Pressure to excel begins early for Hong Kong schoolchildren, whose scholastic future is determined by citywide exams.

moted the idea that only the activity of studying will lead a person to a life of happiness. Studying also had the practical purpose of preparing boys to qualify for the most sought-after jobs in China. Their success brought fame and fortune to the entire family.

Today, Chinese parents are still pushing their children to excel at school. Harold Traver, an associate professor in criminology at Hong Kong University, explains that "In the average Chinese family children are expected to go out and study hard and work hard. There is not the 'do your own thing' looseness that you get in the West."[38]

Hong Kong's young people, though, have a very different view of education and society. They view both skeptically. Around them they observe the increased commercial success of Hong Kong, and often they learn how corruption buys this success openly and goes unpunished. They have learned that education alone will not be enough for them to be successful. About a third of the young people surveyed in a late 1990s Youth Opinion Poll agreed that "in today's society, honesty and integrity will only bring poverty." Twenty percent agreed that if they could solve a problem quickly with a bribe, they would do so. Given this attitude, 70 percent of those polled "feel that the moral standards of young people in Hong Kong have been declining."[39]

Examination Pressure

Most education authorities agree that it is difficult for students to establish a strong ethical foundation in an educational system in which the only criterion for success is high scores on citywide exams. For much of Hong Kong's history, the exam pressure began early in primary school, grades one through six. To get in to a high-rated junior secondary school for grades seven through nine, students needed a high score on the Academic Aptitude Test (AAT) they take in sixth grade.

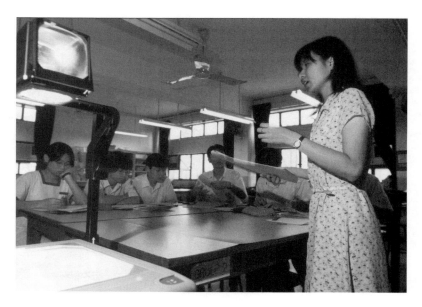

Instructors in Hong Kong teach primarily through dictation and rote memorization, rarely encouraging students' creativity or independent thinking.

Hong Kong students are required to attend school until they are fifteen years old, so almost all students finish junior secondary school. However, education is so important for a comfortable and successful life that almost all students (90 percent) go on to some form of senior secondary school for grades ten and eleven. About 10 percent of these students enroll in technical and vocational schools, which train students for lower-level jobs in industry. Most junior secondary school graduates, however, attend academic-oriented senior secondary schools to prepare for the Hong Kong Certificate of Education Examination (HKCEE).

Taken in the spring of a student's second year in senior secondary school, the HKCEE is the most important public examination for students. About 30 percent will score high enough on the test to enter a two-year school called Form Six and Seven that prepares them to take the citywide university entry exam. All students must take the Chinese, English, and mathematics portions of the HKCEE. They also must sign up for either the science/math or liberal arts sections of the exam. Professor

Ruth Hayhoe, director of the Hong Kong Institute of Education, explains how important these exams are to students' futures and their self-esteem: "Students who do not score well [on the HKCEE and other college entrance exams] . . . [believe] themselves to be a failure in the eyes of their parents and those around them."[40]

As students get closer to taking the HKCEE, they feel the pressure of scoring high enough to continue their education. A survey by the Hong Kong Federation of Youth Groups reported that about 40 percent of the student respondents said they "spent more than six hours on studying per day during the exam period." And "more than 15% said that they had . . . experienced sleeplessness during the exam period."[41]

Teaching for the Tests

The importance of standardized exams is just one aspect of an education system that emphasizes rote memorization and drilling instead of independent thinking. The exams students take for eleven years require mostly recalling facts and formulas they have memorized in school. Most people in Hong Kong want to change this system. In a 1999 youth survey, students ranked "undue emphasis on examination results and the spoon-feeding methods of teaching"[42] as the two major problems with education.

A good example of the spoon-feeding problem is the method used to teach young children English. In primary school classrooms, English skills are mostly graded from dictation exercises. Educator Tsui Hon-Kwong explains that students get approximately eight lessons a week of English, yet they do not learn to converse in the language. He says, "Many children, if they read English at all, can read only silently. Many children cannot read a passage aloud properly even though they can comprehend some of its meaning. These children will never speak the language." Furthermore, when they learn to write English, the letters make no sense. "Letters are nothing more than . . . strokes [as in Chinese writing] that form . . . [English] words."[43] They give no clue to the sounds of the words.

Primary school students have to write out about ten English sentences recited by the teacher. Tsui Hon-Kwong says this "English dictation is what school children dread most. Parents loathe it too. . . . Children hate English from the first month in Primary One onwards because of it."[44] Furthermore, although the textbooks use Western and Asian popular culture for reading assignments, students are never prompted to think critically or discuss the issues. As one eight-year-old student, Cheung Yik-tsai, says, "All we have to do is fill in the blanks."[45]

Extracurricular Activities

So much emphasis on studying and exams does not leave much room for extracurricular activities. They do exist, though. Schools offer a variety of clubs and sports. All schools have clubs in academic areas, such as English, French, mathematics, computers, science, geography, and art. Most secondary schools have debating teams, many of which participate in citywide competitions. Other clubs popular with students relate to music, such as choirs, bands, dance, and guitar. Clubs that train and sponsor traditional Chinese lion dancing are also popular. Many schools also have community service clubs; students in these clubs participate in community activities, visit hospitals, and hold charity drives.

Most schools have limited space, so they are restricted in what they can offer. But most students like to participate in sports. The most popular sport is probably soccer, although several other sports are popular with the students as well. Most schools have track and field, gymnastics, field hockey, and basketball teams. Many of these teams compete in citywide tournaments. In addition, schools sponsor clubs for a variety of sporting activities, such as traditional Chinese kung fu, hiking, and bicycling. Swimming is also popular, given Hong Kong's warm climate and location on the sea.

Hong Kong youths race on a playground.

Curriculum

Most primary students attend half-day sessions between September and June. Because of the overcrowding at the elementary level, Hong Kong has not been able to build enough schools or train teachers fast enough to expand elementary education into full-day sessions. However, the government hopes to have all primary students attending full-day schools by 2006.

In primary school, students study three major subjects that will be the core of their education until they finish schooling: Chinese (written language), English, and mathematics. Then they take general studies courses such as arts and crafts, music, and physical education. In science, a new curriculum emphasizing environmental awareness is now being taught, and most schools are offering some form of computer skill courses as well. Students are also required to take environmental studies and sex education.

The 1997 handover of Hong Kong to China resulted in some additions to the curriculum. One of these, a course called civic education, teaches Chinese history and the laws that govern Hong Kong as a part of China. Furthermore, because Cantonese is spoken in Hong Kong, most people do not understand Mandarin, the official language of China and the language spoken by the majority of Chinese. Since 1997, Mandarin has become a required course at all levels of education. Hong Kong educators hope to train all students to be trilingual—to speak Cantonese, English, and Mandarin.

Secondary schools operate on full-day schedules from September to June. In junior secondary school, the three core subjects (Chinese, English, and math) are continued. In addition, students study Chinese and world history, geography, computer skills, music, art, P.E., Mandarin, and economics. In the ninth grade, students begin concentrating on courses in their academic strengths. Some might take courses in technology, while others take courses in physics, chemistry, and biology. Those stronger in the liberal arts might take courses in speech, as well as continue their history and geography courses. All students will take courses that teach them about civic responsibility, the dangers of drugs, protecting the environment, and the con-

Technical and Vocational Training

Since 1982, Hong Kong's Vocational Training Council (VTC) has offered courses and training in technical and vocational fields. Today the VTC offers courses to more than 120,000 students and workers through its two divisions: the Institute of Vocational Education (IVE) and its job training centers.

In an effort to prepare workers for today's job market, VTC's training boards and committees study the city's manpower needs, establish job specifications, design training programs, and test workers for various levels of skills. Recently VTC created the Chinese Cuisine Training Institute (CCTI), a program to train chefs in Chinese cooking. The CCTI website explains the program's goal, saying "To capitalise on the world's fascination [with] Chinese culture, the CCTI will offer culinary interest courses in the Demonstration Kitchen. It also features a training restaurant serving cuisine and a souvenir shop selling culinary related gift items to enhance the institute's tourist appeal. It is envisioned that the CCTI will enrich the cultural diversity of Hong Kong by actively promoting the deep-rooted heritage and tradition of Chinese culinary art."

sequences of careless sexual activity. And all students continue their study of information technology and computer skills.

The lucky 30 percent who move on from grade eleven into Form Six are drilled for two years in subjects they will be tested on when they take the university entry exam called the Hong Kong Advanced Level Examination (HKALE). Because there are few university openings in Hong Kong, only 18 percent of those who take the HKALE get in to university degree programs each year. Many students use the prestige of attending Form Six to find good jobs at the preprofessional level in business and commerce.

Finishing secondary school does not prepare students well for the competitive job market in Hong Kong. Therefore, the vast majority of students hope to continue schooling after they take the HKCEE. Those who do not score high enough to get in to Form Six do have other options. Many students apply to advanced technical and vocational schools which award them certificates and associate degrees that qualify them to work at midlevel positions in fields such as engineering, business, medicine, law, and social work. The government funds the Hong Kong Institute of Vocational Education (IVE). The IVE has nine different campuses around Hong Kong and teaches a wide range of vocational courses in coordination with industry.

The majority of students who finish senior secondary school, however, enter the workforce. Students with high HKCEE scores can qualify for clerical and entry-level government positions. Others find jobs in businesses such as textiles, restaurants, construction, and shipping.

Higher Education

The students who score in the top 18 percent of the HKALE exam head off to the university. When they finish their degrees, they are able to enter professional careers.

The main tower of the University of Hong Kong is pictured against the backdrop of a high-rise government apartment building.

Until the 1970s, those who wanted a higher education had very few options. There were only two universities in Hong Kong: the University of Hong Kong, formed in 1912, and the Chinese University of Hong Kong, founded in 1963. But with the rapid surge in population during the 1950s and '60s, new higher-education institutions were created every decade beginning in the 1970s. Today the government fully funds eight separate universities. The six newer universities are City University of Hong Kong, Hong Kong Baptist University, Lingnan University, Hong Kong Polytechnic University, Hong

Kong University of Science and Technology, and Hong Kong Institute of Education. Another university, the Open University of Hong Kong, is totally financed by student fees. In addition, there are a few postsecondary institutions funded by private organizations and churches, such as the Francis Hsu College's Centre for Advanced and Professional Studies and Shue Yan College, which offer programs ranging from the preuniversity level to master's degrees. Students must pay for their university education, but those who attend government-sponsored universities usually qualify for financial aid in the form of either grants or loans.

Hong Kong follows the British university system that requires three years of specialized

Universities in Hong Kong

Hong Kong has developed some of the best universities in Asia. Until the 1960s, Hong Kong had only one university, the University of Hong Kong, which was created in 1912 by combining the Medical College founded in 1887 and the newly established Technical Institute. As Hong Kong's demand for higher-skilled workers increased between 1963 and 1997, several new higher-education institutions opened. By 2000, three of Hong Kong's universities were ranked in the top seven in Asia, according to *Asiaweek* magazine: the University of Hong Kong, number three; the Chinese University of Hong Kong, number six; and Hong Kong University of Science and Technology, number seven. In universities that specialize in science and technology, Hong Kong Polytechnic University ranks number twelve. In full-time masters of business administration programs among Asian universities, Chinese University of Hong Kong ranks sixth.

The Hong Kong University of Science and Technology in Kowloon.

study for bachelor degree programs. Hong Kong university degree programs focus on a single major and closely related subjects, rather than a broad range of core courses across academic disciplines. For example, an economics major would take several courses in economics and other courses related to learning how the economy works in such subjects as business, political science, accounting, and statistics. Economic students would not be required to take courses in the liberal arts and humanities (history and literature).

By far, the most popular university degrees are in business and related fields. Almost 25 percent of all university students major in the field of business and management, and a third of these specialize in accounting. Engineering draws about 20 percent of all university students, and science and mathematics account for another 16 percent.

Banding

Because many people contend that Hong Kong's traditional educational system needs to be improved, some changes have already been made, but not everyone is happy about all of them. One of the traditions in Hong Kong's secondary school education that is under attack is "banding." Until 2000, scores on the AAT city-wide exam determined the academic quality of classes for students in secondary school. Band 1 consisted of the top 20 percent of exam takers, and Band 5 came from the lowest 20 percent. Secondary schools then competed for students, and the schools developed reputations depending on the quality of students they attracted.

Hong Kong officials debated the strengths and weaknesses of this policy for years. There have been some suggestions, such as mixing each class with students from each band. However, no final decisions have been made about changing the banding system. Among those who oppose the compromise plan are parents with students in the higher bands. In addition, the students in the top bands tend to support banding. A sixth-form student at prestigious King's College (a secondary school) believes that eliminating banding would not work "because the differences between kids are so large. When I studied with the worst, I was not good. If you have mixed ability schools students will not work so hard."[46]

Discrimination and Placement

One of the more sensitive issues that Hong Kong officials are trying to solve is sex discrimination in education; even the government practices it when placing students into secondary schools. Officials have always adjusted entry scores for junior secondary schools according to gender, arguing that boys mature more slowly than girls. The general practice is to add points to boys' scores to equalize the number of boys and girls who get in to each school. Otherwise, the government maintains, the best schools would have a majority of girl students, and officials claim that a coeducational setting is a better environment for both boys and girls.

Anna Wu Hung-yuk, the chairperson of the Equal Opportunities Commission, disagrees. She argues that the government's policy was a clear example of sex discrimination:

> The Education Department . . . decided to systematically scale up scores for boys and scale down scores for girls. Its argument is essentially that as boys have not maximized their potential by primary [grade] 6, the Department needs to add scores in their favour to give them a chance of maximizing their potential at some point in the future.

Does this not apply to girls too? Well, it wasn't that long ago when girls did not go to school and now that they are doing better in examination results, these results don't seem to count anymore. With an issue as basic as high school education, I do not see how we can avoid putting the case to court. The level playing field must start with basic education for boys and girls.[47]

The issue has not been solved directly. But a new placement procedure being implemented for all Hong Kong students will eliminate most of this problem. This plan involves eliminating the AAT completely and requiring most students to attend the primary school in their home district. When the placement plan was officially announced in early 2000, "moving mania" erupted throughout Hong Kong, because parents wanted their children to attend one of the primary schools that had a reputation for students with high AAT scores; the fact that the test was being eliminated did not matter. Parents complained that if their children were forced to attend schools in their own district, they might not get the best education. Eunic Chan, who had a six-year-old ready to enroll in primary school, complained that "Now your fate is determined at the kindergarten stage. You can't get out of it if you enter a bad school

Since girls generally average higher scores than boys on exams, Hong Kong officials often add points to boys' scores to ensure that an equal number of boys and girls are admitted to the city's best secondary schools.

Hong Kong officials believe that all students should obtain advanced computer skills by the time they finish their education. Therefore, they have begun a program to put computers in every public school. Peter Cordingley of *Asiaweek* writes about St. Joseph's Primary School, chosen in 1998 by the government as one of eight pilot programs to develop information technology (IT) for public schools.

"Ko Po village is about as far from the gleaming towers of Hong Kong's Central district as you can get without leaving the territory. An hour-and-a-half away by train and then taxi, the rural hamlet is accessible only by dirt roads that are lined with low-rise houses, vegetable patches and wild-looking dogs. The children growing up here live a world apart from their cosmopolitan, city-dwelling counterparts. But computers are helping them bridge the divide. The 400 or so students who attend Ko Po's SKH St. Joseph's Primary School have access to some of the most advanced high-tech facilities in Hong Kong. 'We need to give them an advantage because they are rural children,' says teacher Bernard Poon. . . .

The students have their principal to thank. Alan Chan has been aggressive about building a strong computer-education program. Six years ago, when funding was short, he sought out used computers from companies like Reuters. Then in 1998, the private, government-subsidized school was chosen along with nine other primary institutions for the SAR's elite IT pilot program. St. Joseph's now has four servers, a computer lab stocked with 45 Pentium-powered desktops, and three computers in each homeroom—two for the students and one for the teacher. Teaching methods are also Internet-age. Slick Power Point and multi-media presentations have taken the place of the old overhead projector slides. E-mail is a part of daily life, and students listen to Internet radio broadcasts from all over the world. The average St. Joseph's 12-year-old can build his own website. That's the kind of school life that makes the world of Ko Po village much bigger for St. Joseph's students than their parents could have ever imagined."

at the very beginning."[48] Frankie Lam, a father, also admitted that his family "moved to Kowloon Tong [a school district with a good reputation] partly because we wanted our children to enter good schools. Some of my relatives have borrowed our address so their children would apply."[49]

IT

A less controversial issue introduced by government officials is the use of information technology (IT) in the classrooms. This policy, they believe, will allow Hong Kong to continue to be an important economic power, because all businesses and governments in the world will be using computers and communicating over the Internet in the future. All secondary schools and about three hundred primary schools are connected to the Internet. By 2001, each secondary school had about forty computers and each primary school about eighty-two computers. In the future, the government intends to have schools teaching at least 25 percent of their curriculum through IT. To support the use of IT, they have set up training programs for all teachers.

One of the earliest schools to incorporate IT was Hong Kong's St. Paul's Convent Secondary School. An all-girls school, St. Paul's initiative stood out in Hong Kong's traditional Confucian society, one that considers educating girls less important than educating boys. Teacher Law Suiwing, who helped pioneer the IT program, says it is important for girls to gain computer and Internet skills early because "Girls are sometimes told outside of school that they are not suited for subjects like math, science and computers."[50]

Today, in an effort to give Hong Kong's students the best possible education, most schools use Cantonese as the main teaching language. This was not always the case. Until Hong Kong's handover to China in 1997, courses in most secondary schools and in some primary schools were taught in English. However, educational authorities convinced the government that children learn best when taught in their native language. As a result, by 2000, all primary and almost all secondary schools were required to teach all of their courses in Cantonese.

This language switchover in the secondary schools caused many protests from parents concerned that their children would be deprived of mastering English, the most important language used in world commerce. Given Hong Kong's position as one of the world's most important business and trading centers, many parents believe their children can attain fluency in English best by attending schools that teach all courses in English. However, as legislator Tsang Yok-sing points out, "Critics [of the mother tongue policy] have never experienced the agony of having to learn all school subjects in a foreign language [English]."[51]

Whether taught in English or Cantonese, Hong Kong's students today attend schools that seem on the surface very much like those of their parents. The discipline is strict, they wear uniforms, and they rely on memory for many of their important exams. However, beneath the surface, things are different, and those in charge of setting Hong Kong's educational policy hope that the young generation will be able to employ new skills and techniques so they will find success in the world beyond school.

Religion

F ather Charlie Dittmeier, who taught for twelve years at the Roman Catholic Caritas Magdalene School for the deaf in Hong Kong, writes that "Asking a HK [Hong Kong] Chinese person what religion he belongs to often draws a blank because they don't think of themselves as 'belonging' to a group. Instead they are just doing those practices, which others describe as religious, which are a traditional part of Chinese culture."[52] A couple of days of walking around Hong Kong would indeed confirm Dittmeier's observation; the people embrace a great variety of religious practices, from Buddhism and Taoism to traditional folk beliefs based on local legends and ancient superstitions.

Combining Many Beliefs

Daily life in Hong Kong reflects the people's traditional Chinese religious culture. Most people set up small shrines in their apartments to pay tribute to their ancestors. Small shrines can be found outside, too, in alleyways and at corners of buildings. Author Jan Morris writes, "Almost anywhere you may come across the gypsylike little sanctuary of stones, ribbons, red paper and candle stumps which marks a holy site of animism, with a couple of elderly ladies perhaps fiddling around with joss sticks [incense] or pulling cabalistic [symbols or writing with secret meanings] papers out of carrier

The residents of Hong Kong embrace a wide variety of religions and beliefs. Here, worshipers light joss sticks during a festival at a Buddhist temple.

bags."[53] At the small shrines and larger temples, worshipers often light three incense sticks—one for the earth, one for the heavens, and one for humankind. Believers say the smoke carries their wishes to the gods in heaven.

In Hong Kong's more than six hundred temples and shrines, the majority of the city's people practice a combination of Buddhism, Confucianism, and Taoism. Often, a group of people pay respect to Buddha, while a few feet away in the same temple another group prays to a Taoist deity. And when it is time to pay respect to ancestors, most people follow Confucian beliefs. In blending the different aspects of several belief systems, the people of Hong Kong manage to praise the gods and ancestral spirits, who will in turn bring good fortune to the family, thereby allowing the people on earth to live happy and successful lives.

Even those people who practice Christianity in Hong Kong find rituals in the traditional religions to reinforce Christian values. Many Confucian principles, such as having strong family unity, showing respect to other people, and modeling oneself after a successful elder are similar to Christian teachings. One of the major teachings of Buddhism calls for believers to practice the virtue of compassion and charity, which is a major part of Christianity as well. So, Christians in Hong Kong feel comfortable with much of their Chinese religious heritage.

Confucius and Remembering the Ancestors

However, the keystone of Chinese culture is Confucianism. Confucius and his followers taught a system of ethics and behavior that would establish a peaceful and prosperous society. These teachings focused on the family and ancestors. Confucianists believe that ancestors long ago knew how to live in peace with each other better than people do today. Therefore, by paying respect to ancestors and following their ways, people today can learn how to live a better life.

To honor ancestors, those who follow Confucian ideas perform certain rituals. Some rituals can be as simple and private as bowing in front of a small shrine in the home. Others can be as public and universal as the Qing Ming (Clear and Bright) festival, which has been celebrated by the Chinese for more than two thousand years. Held every year on the twelfth day of the third lunar month, Qing Ming is sometimes called the Tomb Sweeping Festival or the Remembrance of Ancestors Day. On this official public holiday, Chinese families go to the cemeteries and pay their respects to their ancestors.

On Qing Ming, Hong Kong authorities tell the city's residents to expect delays on highways and trains because many people travel on this day; public transportation companies even add

Fire in the Hills

Hill fires, a common ritual during the Qing Ming festival, have become such a problem in Hong Kong that the government issues special warnings against them each year. A 2001 government public service notice titled "Public Urged to Help Prevent Hillfires During Ching Ming" appealed to "grave-sweepers to burn offerings and joss sticks in metal containers during the coming Ching Ming Festival, picnic-goers to barbecue at designated sites and to put out fires when they leave, and smokers not to throw cigarette butts in the countryside."

A man and his daughter repaint his parent's grave during the annual Qing Ming festival.

extra buses and trains. Hundreds of thousands of people visit Hong Kong cemeteries on Qing Ming. In addition, more than 200,000 people travel to the Guangzhou area of China, about eighty-four miles north across the South China Sea, where a majority of Hong Kong residents have family roots. Charlie Dittmeier describes one Qing Ming festival he observed during the late 1990s in Hong Kong:

> Hundreds of thousands flock to the cemeteries here and in China to tend to their ancestors' graves, sweeping and cleaning, and then making offerings of fruit [and] rice. . . . The immigration department reported that 280,000 people crossed the land border into China on Friday night [April 1998] at the beginning of the long weekend. There will be an even bigger crush of people tonight when they all return for work tomorrow.[54]

Qing Ming is a time for remembering dead ancestors, but it is also a time for picnics and play. It marks the beginning of spring, so it has a festive atmosphere. The willow trees are budding and everything in Hong Kong is green.

The impact of Buddhism on contemporary life in Hong Kong is illustrated by a story involving Hong Kong's most popular English-language newspaper, the *South China Morning Post*. In the spring of 2001, the newspaper moved in to a new building. Within two weeks, rumors began to circulate that the building was haunted. Food editor Susan Jung, a Chinese American working at the paper, said that when she was washing her hands in the woman's lavatory, she heard someone calling her. But when she turned around, no one was there. Immediately, women started going to the lavatory in groups.

To cleanse the building of its frightening apparitions, newspaper administrators called in two Buddhist monks from the Hong Kong Bodhi Siksa Society. In the lobby, the monks set up an altar to cleanse the office of the ghosts, a common practice for haunted buildings in Hong Kong. In her article "Ghost-Ridding Ceremony Performed at Post," writer Niki Law says,

"Then the monks began a prayer and proceeded to tour the office, chanting and splashing water from a cup with a pomelo leaf, known to drive away bad luck.

'The prayer's purpose is to cast away the powers of the spirit and cleanse the office,' said monk Yiliu.

'This kind of ceremony is very common, about 14 to 18 cases a year, as many offices have experienced similar instances of haunting in the past,' reverend [monk] Sik Wing-sing added."

Children and adults alike crowd the parks to fly elaborately designed kites; some are cut and painted to flutter like butterflies with wings, and others to fly like goldfish with swaying tails.

Buddhism

Like Confucianism, Buddhism plays an important role in the lives of the majority of people in Hong Kong. Buddhists trace their religion back to Siddhartha Gautama, a young prince who lived in northern India during the sixth century B.C. Siddhartha noticed that selfishness and craving for pleasure led people into a self-centered lifestyle that caused everyone to suffer. As a result, he concluded that while people are alive they can escape the sources of suffering by looking outward to help others. Buddhists believe that at this point Siddhartha received enlightenment, the true meaning of life. Therefore, he is called the "Buddha," or the Enlightened One.

Like all religions, Buddhism changed over the centuries. Different schools of thought developed as the religion spread into Tibet, Southeast Asia, and China. As it mixed with local superstitions and religions, a new form of Buddhism evolved that added on a priesthood (monks) and places of worship (temples). This new form, called Mahayana Buddhism, teaches that there are heavens and hells and that people can be rewarded or punished in any of these for many centuries. This form of Buddhism also teaches that the individual spirit, if not perfected, goes through an endless series of rebirths into different levels of heaven and hell and back into the world.

The people of Hong Kong embraced this religious philosophy and made it part of their culture. They built temples and altars where they could practice these beliefs. Jan Morris describes a typical Buddhist temple crowded with people who stop by to offer short prayers for good luck or health. Inside the temples, Morris writes, "there will be the caretakers at their dusky desks, surrounded by holy texts and pictures, and before the gaudy altars women will be shaking the *chim*, the box of bamboo fortune sticks, while incense smokes, bells tinkle and the blackened god-images [of Buddha] peer down from their altars."[55]

One of the most popular Buddhist temples in Hong Kong is Man Fat Tze, located in the hills overlooking the town of Sha Tin, in the New Territories. Here, thousands of Buddhists climb about five hundred stone steps to the main Man Fat Tze altar to see some of the thirteen thousand statues of Buddha in residence there, each one gilded and each face carved with a different pose, or to view the mummified body of Yuet Kai, the monk who founded the monastery in 1950. Morris describes the mummy: "[He] sits

A gilded statue of Buddha adorns a shrine at a Hong Kong temple; Buddhism has played an important role in shaping Hong Kong culture.

bold upright forever in a tall glass case, covered in gold leaf and looking alert but blotched with what I assume to be preservative."[56]

Another popular temple is Po Lin, Precious Lotus Monastery, on Lantau Island. Located near the top of the 3,064-foot Lantau Peak, the second highest point in Hong Kong, the monastery offers a famous outdoor bronze statue of Buddha built by the Chinese Space Agency and opened for the public in 1993. Visitors must climb 264 steps to get to the base, which was modeled after the Temple of Heaven in Beijing. Inside the statue is a three-story hall with a large bell engraved with Buddhist pictures and scripture.

Because of the widespread practice of Buddhism in Hong Kong, the government declared Buddha's birthday, the eighth day of the fourth lunar calendar month, as a national holiday. On May 22, 1999, the Hong Kong government celebrated this holiday officially for the first time. The center of the activities was the display of one of Siddhartha's teeth, flown in from a monastery in Beijing. More than 300,000 people visited the Hong Kong Coliseum, where the tooth was showcased, to pay their respects. Throughout Hong Kong, lion dances and parades were held during the twelve-day celebration.

Taoism

Another major religion in Hong Kong is Taoism. More than a dozen different Taoist groups practice in Hong Kong. Each group stresses a distinct aspect of Taoist beliefs, but members of all groups believe in a single core of ideas. The Taoists believe in a large number of deities, most of whom were once human. When living on earth, these future deities performed fantastic feats that benefited groups and communities. After they died, their stories circulated and

Dozens of large, coiled incense rods hang from the ceiling of the Taoist Man Mo Temple on Hong Kong Island.

became the core of legends. Some of these gods are known only in certain cities or regions, while others are honored throughout Asia.

A few popular deities are recognized by Chinese all over the world. Two of these are Kuan Ti and Man Cheong, who are the center of worship in the Man Mo Temple on Hong Kong Island. Peter Lok describes the temple's statues of these two gods: "The green robed god on the left [side of the temple's main altar] is Kuan Ti, the God of War, and protector of policemen, the military. . . . The red robed god on the right is Man Cheong, the God of Literature, and protector of civil servants."[57] During the many Taoist festivals, these statues are placed in sedan chairs and paraded through the streets of Hong Kong Island.

Built before British colonization in the 1840s, Man Mo Temple is a small, pagoda-type building that sits almost unnoticed beneath high skyscrapers. However, as Jan Morris writes, inside "is a dimly lit, smoky, gilded, cluttered and cheerful distillation [a good example] of . . . a Chinese temple."[58] Hanging in the center of the temple are huge coiled rods of incense several feet in height. People pay money to keep this incense burning because they believe that incense is food for the spirits of ancestors.

Tin Hau

Because of Hong Kong's location on the sea, the Taoist goddess Tin Hau, protector of seafarers, is popular in Hong Kong. The legend originated in China's Fujian province north of Hong Kong. There are different stories that account for Tin Hau's elevation as a deity. However, all the legends claim she could heal illnesses and predict dangers at sea so sailors could travel safely. One story claims she was the daughter of a rich government official, while another says she was from a poor fishing family. Peter Lok offers this account of the legend:

> Tin Hau was a girl in a poor fishing family. One day she dreamed her father and two brothers were drowning at sea in a terrible storm and she began to drag them to shore. Her mother woke her up before she was finished though. [When they arrived home] the two brothers swore that a beautiful woman took them to safety, but her father unfortunately drowned. She was promoted to Queen of Heaven in 1683 after helping the Chinese navy regain control over Taiwan.[59]

Various stories of Tin Hau's accomplishments spread, and fishermen carried these tales to the islands off of China's coast. By the seventeenth century, she was accepted as a major goddess by fishermen in Hong Kong. Today, more than 250,000 people in Hong Kong honor Tin Hau at more than forty temples. Every year, a festival is held on the twenty-third day of the third lunar month to honor her birthday. During this festival, fishermen pray for good weather, safety, and large catches during the following fishing season. Hundreds of boats colorfully decorated with red flags inscribed with praises for Tin Hau sail the shorelines, and parades and lion dances are held throughout Hong Kong.

Feng Shui

These three traditions—Confucianism, Buddhism, and Taoism—form the basis for the religious culture in Hong Kong and throughout China. Furthermore, they overlap and merge with ancient religious beliefs, legends, and superstitions.

Long before there were formal religions in China, the people tried to explain life and events around them. They believed that the universe was made up of three parts: heaven, earth, and humans. On earth, an invisible life force or energy called "chi" influenced people's lives. Chi should flow smoothly like a winding river. If chi flowed too fast or too slowly, then it became bad energy. To ensure the flow of positive chi, the Chinese devised the theory of feng shui (wind and water), which became one of the many beliefs of Taoism.

Feng shui is very popular in Hong Kong. This philosophy refers to the idea that wind and water are the basic forces in nature. Over time, they change the shape of the land and, in turn, the way people live. The early Chinese, then, devised feng shui as a theory of placing buildings and other objects in positions that did not interfere with the natural flow of wind and water. Author Lillian Too says that "Almost everyone believes in feng shui here [Hong Kong], from tycoon to most humble street vendor."[60] It applies not only to locations for buildings but also to the placement of doors, windows, mirrors, furniture, and every other object in a building. According to *Passport Hong Kong*, a popular guide for doing business in the city, when planning a building, its "interior must be aligned to prevent bad spirits from slipping in. The strategic positioning of a mirror can deflect or divert them; doors must never be in a straight line."[61]

When builders in Hong Kong do not consult feng shui experts, Hong Kong residents get upset. An example of this occurred with the enormous Bank of China Tower, completed in 1990. Chinese authorities commissioned world-famous Chinese American architect I. E. Pei to design the building. What he came up with has been a major controversy ever since. The building is situated in a good location, but as *Time* journalist Howard G. Chua-Eoan reported, from the time construction on the Bank of China Tower began, people in the area worried, contending that "the triangular elements of the structure spell[ed] bad luck. Reason: the acute pointy edges would slice through the yin-yang, or cosmic balance, thus pricking and angering unwary spirits, who would then direct their anger at buildings toward which the triangles pointed."[62]

To avert such controversy, most builders choose to consult feng shui experts. For example, British architect Norman Foster brought in feng shui specialists to help him design the forty-seven-story Hong Kong Shanghai Bank in 1985. The feng shui experts advised Foster on the angles and directions of almost all the construction in the building, from the position of the elevators to the two stone lions sitting on the outside of the building. Furthermore, as journalist Glenda Winders explains, "Two cranes that were set atop the building for cleaning purposes were never removed because they resembled cannons that could shoot negative energy back eastward toward the bank's most ardent rival, the Bank of China."[63]

Lucky Numbers

Choosing lucky numbers for addresses, how many rooms in a home, even license numbers, is another aspect of feng shui to which Hong Kong residents ascribe. The reason behind the choice of numbers lies mostly in the sound of words. In Cantonese, the same word might have dozens of meanings depending on slight variations of tone. The word for the number four, for example, sounds the same as the word for death. As a result, many buildings avoid using number four. As Charlie Dittmeier explains, "One new skyscraper recently completed in Hong Kong has 62 floors, according to the architect's plans. But if you enter the elevator to go to the top floor, you have to press '70'. . . . All floors with 4s (4, 14, 24, 34, 44, 54, 64, 74) were eliminated to cater to the superstitious who would not want to work or do business on a floor associated with death. And the 13th floor was also omitted to cater to western superstitions."[64]

On the other hand, the word for the number nine sounds like the word for eternity, so nine is a lucky number. Many people try to find ways to use this number in their lives. Hong Kong's government takes advantage of number superstition to raise money by auctioning off license plates each year. In 1994, for instance, Albert Yeung, a business tycoon, bought the plate numbered "9" for $1.7 million HK (about $217,977 US).

Other lucky numbers include three, which sounds like the word for life, and eight, which sounds like "prosperity." The Bank of China Tower picked one of the luckiest days of the

The Bank of China Tower is considered by many to be an unlucky building because its triangular design elements do not conform to the principles of feng shui.

century to open its doors, 8-8-88, and restaurants sometimes offer dinners for $88 (HK). And at the race track, many people depend on these lucky numbers to pick horses.

Fortune-Telling

In addition, residents of Hong Kong, and Chinese in general, believe that people on earth can gain wisdom and ensure good luck by communicating with those who exist in heaven or other spiritual worlds. They also believe that a few special people on earth can help interpret signs from those in the spiritual world. As a result, Hong Kong residents consult spirits or look for signs to answer many of the questions they face daily. Some people might want to know if they should pursue a business deal. Parents may want insight about naming a child. Couples might want advice about their marriage or when to take a vacation.

Whatever their questions, the most popular method of discovering one's future in Hong Kong is by asking fortune-tellers, and one way to do this is with "fortune sticks," common in both Buddhist and Taoist temples. To use the sticks, a Hong Kong resident would go to a temple or shrine and pick up a *chim*, a bamboo canister of wooden sticks. After asking his or her question, the person will shake the canister until a stick falls out. This stick will have a number on it. The person then takes the stick to a fortune-teller in the temple who interprets the meaning by matching the number with prewritten fortunes. Obviously, these fortunes offer broad, vague answers and can be used for hundreds of different questions. However, the fortune-teller interprets the answer for the individual.

Another popular means of getting one's fortune told is going to a palm reader, many of whom work at street markets. Palm readers analyze both the lines and features of the hand. Palm readers also study a person's face to supplement the palm reading, believing there are forty-eight eye patterns and eight facial shapes that reveal character and fortune.

Western Religions

Despite how widespread those ancient religions and traditions are, more than a half-million Hong Kong residents practice Christianity in hundreds of churches. Missionaries from Great Britain brought Christianity to Hong Kong in the 1840s, and today, Christians make up such a

A fortune-teller performs a palm reading at a Kowloon temple. Consulting fortune-tellers is a popular practice in Hong Kong.

A Hong Kong mall is decked out with a large tree and other decorations during the Christmas season, just one example of the Christian influence throughout the city.

large portion of the city's population that after Hong Kong's return to China, the government retained the two major Christian holidays—Christmas and Easter—as public holidays.

Christmas has become particularly popular in Hong Kong. In December, buildings and malls throughout the city are covered with decorations. Randall van der Woning describes the scene at one shopping center, the Sha Tin Plaza: "A giant white two-storey cake, festooned with huge strawberries, candy canes, cookies, gingerbread men, Christmas trees, and giant purple ornaments nearly the size of bowling balls, surrounded by massive purple and gold cones hanging three stories down from the ceiling"[65] adorn the mall.

Although Christmas decorations are quite common, the Christian influence in the city is most obvious in education and social services. Churches operate three postsecondary colleges (Chung Chi College at the Chinese University of Hong Kong, Hong Kong Baptist University, and Lingnan University) and nearly one thousand secondary schools, primary schools, kindergartens, and nurseries. Beyond the classroom, churches also work in health and community welfare. There are more than a dozen hospitals, scores of clinics, and hundreds of social service organizations serving Hong Kong residents, including children's homes, homes for the elderly, schools for the deaf and blind, and centers that train the mentally handicapped and disabled.

Whether Christian, Buddhist, or Taoist, the residents of Hong Kong are a people who successfully incorporate religion into their daily lives. In temples, on street corners, and in homes, they blend organized religion, traditional beliefs, and Confucian philosophy into a system that allows them to realize and promote their culture's most sacred goals: respecting ancestral spirits and living a happy, successful life.

Earning a Living

Hong Kong resident Joseph Yu works four jobs to support his family of four; they live in a 120-square-foot room. That's the down side. The "up" side is that his hard work has made him wealthy—he co-owns a Mercedes and will move in to a much more comfortable house when one becomes available. Yu used to drive a taxi full-time, but found the expenses too high. So he branched out. As author Simon Winchester reports, Yu "is a hospital telephone operator several nights a week, teaches kung fu to children, owns a chauffeur service with his sister, and fills in driving a taxi when needed."[66]

Obsession with Work

Yu's work ethic is so common in Hong Kong that it could be called the dominant character trait of the people who live there. Most adults work six days a week, and many, like Joseph Yu, work more than one job. As one resident told *Time* magazine in 1980, "With one job I was not tired. So I took a second job, and now I make a lot more money. That is important in Hong Kong."[67]

Many outsiders wonder what drives people in Hong Kong to work so hard. Even before the British colonialists brought their "capitalist" theories of free enterprise, the Cantonese had an ancient saying: *"Moh ching, moh meng"* (No money, no life). As a result, owning a business is the single most important dream of most young people in Hong Kong. In surveys, the majority of secondary students say owning their own business is their first preference for work. And in the major universities almost 25 percent of all students major in business and management.

Elizabeth Chin of the Catholic Immigration Center in Toronto, Canada, describes this intense work ethic as a survival technique. She writes,

Hong Kong workers have a strong work ethic; many people work long hours at more than one job.

Hong Kong people—whether they are professionals, street hawkers, government employees or shopkeepers—work at a very fast pace. They see it as the only way to survive. . . . Business people make deals during ten-minute ferry rides across the harbour. Tourists notice that even the escalators of the underground mass transit system move faster than they do in the west."[68]

The First Economic Revolution

In 1949, when communism swept through mainland China, more than 1 million refugees flooded into British-controlled Hong Kong. These refugees provided what journalist Rahul Jacob describes as "plenty of cheap labor and business savvy. . . . The exodus from China became a huge factor in Hong Kong's swift industrialization: the 1,478 manufacturing establishments in 1950 multiplied to 16,507 by 1970."[69]

Although some of the refugees came from middle-class backgrounds, the vast majority were poor, often peasants from south China. Most of Hong Kong's jobs were in manufacturing, assembling watches and sewing clothing, and the hundreds of thousands of poor, unskilled peasants provided an endless supply of cheap labor. These businesses, commonly lo-

Refugees from Communist China at the border of British-controlled Hong Kong in 1949. The influx of 1 million refugees played a major role in the rapid industrialization of the city.

Many of the wealthy families in Hong Kong are descendants of those who left Communist China. Several fled from Shanghai, a city in eastern China. One family was lead by K. N. Godfrey Yeh. In his article, "From Father to Son: One Company's Dilemma," journalist Rahul Jacob describes Yeh's success story. Yeh had started a construction company called Hsin Chong, in Shanghai before World War II. In 1939 he opened an office in Hong Kong, but when the Communists took control of China, Yeh moved everything to Hong Kong.

"[The] Yehs and Hsin Chong were smack in the middle of this prodigious effort [to build housing for Hong Kong's millions during the 1970s and '80s]. Banking [depending] on sizeable, repeat contracts from the government, . . . Yeh introduced an expensive, large-panel metal formworks system that made construction faster and improved the quality of a building's finish. The high cost cuts into profits initially, but the device makes up for it by improving ef-ficiency and slashing labor costs. It gave Hsin Chong an advantage as the government kept building giant complexes to keep up with Hong Kong's fast-growing population.

Since the late 1970s, Hsin Chong has built more than 20 public housing estates. During that time Yeh has moved the firm upmarket by progressively expanding its services beyond simple construction to include design, fire safety and building management. Hsin Chong has essentially become a one-stop shop, even for such complicated structures as hospitals. Says Hu Fa-Kuang, whose firm supplies elevators and escalators to Hsin Chong: 'When there is a new idea, they are usually the first to introduce it.'"

The company was also involved in the construction of the new airport, the thirty-eight-story World Trade Center, and the Hong Kong University of Science and Technology. By 2000, Hsin Chong was worth more than $350 million and employed more than a thousand workers.

cated in rooms or parts of rooms in old buildings in back alleys off the major roadways, used fewer than ten workers: and often most or all the workers were related to each other.

The output from these small endeavors was nothing short of phenomenal. During the 1960s, Hong Kong's economy grew rapidly. As historian Frank Welsh writes, Hong Kong became "stable and increasingly affluent"; wages "rose by 50 per cent, and the percentage of households with incomes of less than $400 [1960s value] (which could be regarded as fairly acute poverty) fell from well over 50 per cent to 16 per cent."[70]

Rags to Middle Class

As a result of the growing economy and the people's work ethic, Hong Kong residents underwent a transformation from poor to middle class. Forty-year-old Chong Shiu Fan is a typical example of this. Fan always worked, even as a child, to help her family. Her mother sold fruit on the street, and her father fixed boat engines. Journalist Edward Gargan describes Fan's determination: "Usually before sunrise, . . . in knee-high rubber boots, [she] clomps from her tiny apartment across the street to her storefront stacked with fish tanks, tubs of shrimps and

Although the clothing industry remains a major employer in Hong Kong, many factories are moving to mainland China where labor costs are lower.

abalone and trays of rockfish on ice" and opens her store, Kin Wah Fresh Seafood. She has "intense black eyes [that] seem larger under her cropped hair. Her hands are toughened by a life of labor. [Along] Wanchai Road, a twisted lane hedged by vegetable stores, poultry stalls and fish vendors, she is known as Big Eyes."[71] Fan's store is truly a family business. Her husband handles the business decisions and drives his truck to wholesale markets to buy the fish. Her son did not want to continue in school, so he is in charge of preparing the fish to be displayed on the racks.

Other workers, like waiter Pang Hon Ming, spend so many hours a week on the job that they have little free time to spend with their families. Pang arrived in Hong Kong as an infant with his parents, who fled the mainland in 1950. Pang told journalist Gargan, "I leave home at 5:30 and I get here [to work] about 6:35 and work until 2:30 in the afternoon. Then I'm off. I start again at 6 and work until 10:30. Then I go home. I only get two days off every month, so I work 28 days a month. The law is you're supposed to get four days off a month, but most restaurants only give two."[72]

The Second Economic Revolution

With the personal drive and tenacity of people like Chong Shiu Fan and Pang Hon Ming, Hong

Kong's economy flourished. By the late 1970s, Hong Kong's economy had expanded and progressed so rapidly that a second economic revolution occurred; this time, there was a dramatic shift in production from manufacturing products to providing services, such as banking and insurance. By 2000, the Hong Kong government reported that almost 2 million of Hong Kong's 3.5 million workers were employed in the service portion of the economy, jobs that involved everything from import and export to communications and tourism. Jobs in banking, insurance, real estate, and business services alone grew from 4.6 percent of the service jobs in 1980 to 14.5 percent in 1999. And tourism, always an important industry in Hong Kong, had its best year ever in 2000, recording more than 13 million visitors.

Companies that manufacture products such as textiles, toys, electronics, plastics, jewelry, and watches, on the other hand, declined. In all, manufacturing employed about 244,500 workers at the end of 1999, only about 7 percent of Hong Kong's workforce. Today, the clothing industry remains the major employer in manufacturing, with almost 55,000 workers. However, since the late 1980s, owners have been moving their clothing factories to the mainland because labor costs are five to six times lower there than in Hong Kong. The shift of these lower-skilled jobs to mainland China takes jobs away from the lesser-skilled workers in Hong Kong. As a result, the unemployment rate in Hong Kong rose to a new high of more than 7 percent in 1998.

Women in the Workplace

These low-skilled jobs have traditionally been held by women. So when owners move their factories to mainland China, Hong Kong women are usually the first to lose their jobs. Between 1986 and 1991, for example, 64 percent of all workers who lost their jobs were women. According to a report presented to the Hong Kong Women Workers Association by Linda To, "Women who have remained in the declining manufacturing sector experience many problems. They are paid substandard wages—most work on a piece-work basis and cannot earn an adequate living due to the reduction of work."[73]

Thousands of Hong Kong women participate in piecework or outwork jobs, working independently for contractors and getting paid by the number of products they can make at home. According to writer William Keng Mun Lee, "Traditionally, the garment, plastics, and toy industries have been the major users of outwork contracting to meet changing export demand. In recent years, assembly work in the electronics industry has also found a place in the informal world of outwork."[74]

However, with the shift of much of the lower-skilled work to factories on mainland China, even outwork jobs are disappearing in Hong Kong. As a result, more and more women are unable to find work. Furthermore, unemployment affects women past the age of thirty most because the few employers who are willing to hire women generally hope to hire women in their twenties who can make do with lower salaries.

Besides a changing economy, women are also influenced by traditional social values that pressure them to leave the workforce voluntarily in their midthirties to tend to household work, especially to take care of their children. A government survey in 1993 indicated that nearly 50 percent of the women who left the workforce did so to return full-time to take care of their children and homes. According to a report prepared by the Citizens Party, a group that investigates and publishes information on Hong Kong politics and society, "For many women in Hong Kong, having a child and having a job are still seen as mutually exclusive."[75]

One reason women leave the workforce to care for their families is Hong Kong's inadequate child care system. Child care centers are expensive, and although the government does give financial aid to needy families, according to one study, the aid covers only 10 percent of the families who need assistance. Furthermore, many families who can afford the price of child care must wait a year or more for openings at child care centers. As a result of high expenses and the scarcity of child care centers, thousands of mothers work either part-time or not at all so they can care for their children and family.

Overcoming the Odds

Despite these concerns, tens of thousands of women have overcome the city's traditional discriminatory practices. They work most often in travel agencies, public relations, and sales and are usually highly independent and nontraditional in their attitudes. They often defy the system, but frequently sacrifice the customary life as wife and mother. For example, more and more Hong Kong women are delaying marriage or choosing not to marry at all. In fact, by the mid-1990s, almost 30 percent of women with professional careers chose to remain single. For many career women, "being single at age 30, or 35, or older, is not a stigma; it's a status symbol," says reporter Susan Berfield. "These women won't settle for men who don't inspire them or nurture their aspirations. A good husband, they say, can keep pace with his wife without stepping on her toes. These are women who are used to having their own space. They want a man with maturity, not just money; someone who will be a companion, not a guardian."[76]

Successful women professionals are usually well educated and come from families with money. Some of these women, like Jennifer Liu, have also benefited from their knowledge of computers and Internet technology. A twenty-six-year-old architecture student, Liu began her apartment-listing service online with the $10,000 prize money she won for a furniture design contest. She also benefited from family connections. Her father, a major Hong Kong banker, introduced her to the son of a Hong Kong billionaire family who decided to invest in her company. Her company, Pp.com, was recently valued at $65 million. Liu says, "[The son, Benjamin Fok,] invited me and my business partner to play golf. What I admired was that he wasn't inviting my dad to play golf. And my dad didn't go to the meeting."[77]

Although women in Hong Kong are often still bound by discriminatory traditions, many, like these female stock traders, have managed to become successful professionals.

Successful Single Women

One of the most famous Hong Kong multi-millionaires was Aw Boon How, who made his fortune during the 1930s from the production and sales of Tiger Balm, a menthol ointment used to relieve aching muscles. Aw Boon How built a large public garden in which he placed concrete statues representing different events and figures from traditional Chinese religions. He also owned a group of Hong Kong newspapers. Aw Boon How's daughter, Sally Aw Sian, took over part of the family business when she was twenty-three years old. In the feature "Why Women Stay Single," correspondent Susan Berfield describes the success of Sally Aw Sian.

"Sally Aw Sian, 64, . . . began [in the 1950s] with the family home in Hong Kong, the then-ailing *Sing Tao* newspaper group and a modest piece of Hong Kong real estate. Since then she has built a business empire estimated to be worth billions. Among her accomplishments was to quickly transform *Sing Tao*, the group's Hong Kong–based flagship, into one of the territory's most profitable newspapers. In 1978 she began beaming her pages via satellite to Chinese communities around the world, making it the first truly international Chinese newspaper. In 1971, she became the first Asian to head the august International Press Institute [an organization begun in 1950 to promote world peace through fair and unbiased news reporting]. Though her father was a well-known Kuomintang [Taiwan's ruling party at the time] supporter, she was able to open several ventures in China as well. A sign of her importance was demonstrated on her first trip to Beijing in 1992, when she was granted audiences with [Communist] party chief Jiang Zemin and Premier Li Peng.

The secret to her success, she insists, is simple: 'It was all a matter of patiently working with the numbers, cutting costs, looking into details and being on the job every day.' And spending wisely. She has a Rolls Royce but usually drives a Volvo."

The Technology Revolution

Like Jennifer Liu, thousands of Hong Kong women and men have converted to what one writer calls the "dot com religion." In fact, since the late 1990s, the government has promoted the idea that Hong Kong must become a world leader in information technology in order to maintain its position as one of the world's major economic powers. This rapid transformation to a high-tech economy was the subject of an address by U.S. consul general Michael Klosson in 1999:

One of the things that has changed dramatically since I last lived here is the economy. When I left Hong Kong in 1972, it was a city dominated by low-cost manufacturing, where hard work and cheap labor gave Hong Kong a competitive edge. I returned to a city dominated by property, banking, retail and other services, where sophistication and expertise provide the edge in a high-cost environment. And, judging from all the studies I have read, speeches I have heard and discussion I have encountered these past two months, the wheel is again turning. Hong Kong is now seeking to chart its future through the portals of the knowledge-based economy of bits and bytes.[78]

This high-tech revolution, like most major economic changes everywhere, has come with

Computer engineers keep an eye on operations at iLink.net, one of Hong Kong's many Internet companies.

a price: unemployment, around 5 percent in 2001. The people most often affected by the rise in Hong Kong's unemployment are middle-aged workers without updated skills. Most businesses in Hong Kong need software engineers, information technology specialists, and Web designers. Today, jobs involving computation, design, and sales work use computers as well. However, middle-aged workers finished their education before computers were popular; therefore, they lack the skills to perform these new jobs. According to Professor Sunny Kai-sun Kwong, an economist at the Chinese University of Hong Kong, "the transition of the economy from manufacturing to service, and further to knowledge-intensive activities threatens to remove [unskilled workers] further and further away from the core. This group is also hard to retrain."[79]

Another group affected by the increase in technology-intensive jobs is young people who finished their education before the government's recent push for computer education in the schools. About 10 percent of the people in the fifteen- to twenty-four-year-old age group are unemployed, many because they lack the skills required for high-tech jobs. Most of these young people completed the mandatory schooling through the age of fifteen, or grade nine, but scored low on examinations that would qualify them for more advanced education. As a result, they seek full-time work but find that there are not many jobs available to them in the new economy.

The unemployed, both the young and middle-aged, often become part of the growing number of poor in Hong Kong. As many as 1 million people might fall into this category.

Reporter Yulanda Chung writes that "Many [of Hong Kong's poor] are low-skilled laborers who have been sidelined by the rush of manufacturers relocating to China, where overheads are cheaper." [80]

The middle-aged unemployed have few choices. A few are able to complete retraining programs and find new jobs. However, most do not. Many of the middle-aged unemployed rely on family for assistance, and those who work part-time work at low-paying jobs. Among the young people who are unable to find work, a large number turn to crime and drugs.

With information technology dominating the world marketplace in the twenty-first century, Hong Kong officials are determined to increase their efforts to train workers for jobs in computer and Internet technology. The people of Hong Kong have shown in the past a remarkable ability to adapt to challenges. And those accomplishments are a natural product of their passion for work.

Enjoying Life

E ven in their fast-paced society, the people of Hong Kong find time to relax and have fun. After long days at work, adults come home to unwind in front of their favorite television shows. When not working on homework, young people watch MTV or listen to the latest Canto–pop music stars singing love ballads. On holidays and Sundays, families and friends flock to amusement parks.

The most popular festivities for Hong Kong residents, however, are the many celebrations connected with their Chinese heritage, when families gather together for large meals and to play mahjong, a game using dice and tiles. Three of the most important festivals in Hong Kong are the Chinese New Year, the Dragon Boat Festival, and the Mid-Autumn Festival. These festivals are among the many official holidays celebrated in Hong Kong every year. In just one thirty-day span ending on May 1, 2001, for example, the holidays included two related to Buddhism, three to Christianity, and one to workers.

Chinese New Year

The most important time of the year for the people of Hong Kong is the Chinese New Year. The actual day varies each year but always falls between January 20 and February 20. The new moon during that period marks the beginning of the new year, a time to put aside the past year's problems and start fresh.

Preparations for the New Year's celebration begin before New Year's Eve. People clean their houses, setting the tone for "starting over" with a clean slate. Old debts and grievances are forgiven, so everyone can begin life anew. On New Year's Eve, families stay up until midnight to welcome the new year. Those who can afford it go out to restaurants with friends. Others stay home for dinner and watch the celebrations on television. Then, on New Year's Day, everyone is on the move, taking buses and trains back and forth to visit relatives. They greet each other with the expression *"Kung Hei Fat Choy,"* Cantonese for "Happiness and Prosperity in the New Year."

The Chinese New Year period is the heaviest travel time of the year; more than 7 million people exit and enter Hong Kong. People pack the streets, carrying presents wrapped in bright red colors, for red is considered the color of prosperity. And children usually receive from adult relatives a dozen or more *lai see*, red envelopes with bills ranging from HK$20 (about $2.56 US) to HK$100 (about $12.80 US).

Food is another major part of the New Year's celebration. The biggest family meal actually precedes New Year's Eve. This meal is supposed to impress Tsao Kwan, the Kitchen God, so he will go back to heaven and tell the family's departed ancestors that their descendants are living well and following traditions. At the dinner, residents offer special sticky candy to Tsao Kwan to convince him to speak only "sweet words" about the family.

Families eat other foods to bring them good luck as well. One of these, described by the Hong Kong Tourist Association, is "Chinese dumplings and eggs, [which] imply wealth, since they have the shape of ancient Chinese [money]. [In addition,] abalone represents abundance, oysters are good for business, mushrooms mean 'growing opportunity'. . . , fish means 'surplus', . . . and pork signals 'prosperity'. Almost everyone has a sip of Jiao (usually hard liquor), since the word is pronounced the same as the word for 'longevity' in Chinese."[81]

Then on New Year's Day, the family sits down to a nine-course meal. (Nine is a lucky number.) After dinner, the family gathers for games and other activities. Randall van der Woning writes that all around him, "In nearly every flat, you will find a game of Mah Jong in progress."[82]

Spring Festival

Chinese New Year also begins a fifteen-day celebration known as Spring Festival. During this time, flower markets flourish. Kumquat trees and narcissus flowers are displayed around the city, and lilies and peonies appear in people's homes. Peach blossoms are popular because they are believed to bring good luck in male-female relationships. Red scrolls with large black calligraphy of the characters that mean happiness, prosperity, and long life are also hung inside homes, in windows, and on buildings. Randall van der Woning explains some of the customs he observed while participating with his wife and her family's celebration of the 2000 Spring Festival:

One of the most popular purchases is a tall tangerine tree planted in a pot, which signifies long-lasting relationships. For married people, it also means the marriage will be fruitful. . . . When visiting, you stand in line to greet your elders with a hearty Kung Hei Fat Choy (prosperous wishes), and follow it up with Long Mah Jing San (energetic as a dragon and a horse), or for the younger relatives, Bo Bo Go Sing (promoted to a higher position).[83]

Participants perform a Chinese drum dance during a parade celebrating the Chinese New Year.

A Hong Kong man puts up colorful lanterns at a fair booth in preparation for the city's annual lantern festival.

The Spring Festival peaks on the fifteenth day after New Year's with a lantern festival. During the festival, lanterns of every imaginable shape and color hang from tree branches, in windows, and from sidewalk awnings. Some are so tiny they can be carried in a person's hand; others are gigantic and block out much of a window. The lanterns display artistic scenes from traditional China, legendary animals, good luck charms, fancy calligraphy, popular singers and movie stars, rockets, boats, airplanes—just about anything that can be illustrated or photographed. Especially popular are lanterns shaped like carp (a symbol of wisdom and bravery), lobsters (a symbol of laughter and fun), and butterflies (a symbol of long life).

Dragon Boat Festival (Tuen Ng)

The Tuen Ng, or Dragon Boat Festival, ranks with the Spring Festival as one of Hong Kong's most popular yearly celebrations. The Dragon Boat Festival is actually two events: one made up of local competitors who hold a series of races beginning in late May or early June and a second international race with teams coming from around the world to compete.

Each local race draws up to a hundred teams from foreign corporations located in Hong Kong, city businesses, banks, local universities, sports clubs, police and firemen groups, and other organizations, and as many as ten thousand spectators. The major racing distances are 1,000

Dragon Boat Racing

In Hong Kong, the annual Dragon Boat Festival is a public holiday held in late May or early June. Although tens of thousands of spectators attend the boat races for entertainment, the village fishermen follow their centuries-old customs of blessing and decorating the dragon boats before the race and then storing the boats when the races are finished. In "The History of Dragon Boat Racing," the Dragon Boat Association of Edmonton, Canada, explains the ceremonies that precede and follow the races.

"When a village builds a new dragon boat a Taoist priest will [bless it to] give it life. With a bell in one hand and a sword in the other he plunges the sword in a Fu Zhou, a paper bearing 'MAGIC' CHARACTERS. The priest then touches the dragon's head, tail and the drum on the boat with a sword. Paper [fake] 'money' is burned and sand is sprinkled on the dragon's head. A community leader dots the eyes of the dragon and the eyes are later drawn on in detail in red paint.

The ceremonies are believed to ward off evil, sanctify the boats and imbue them with the strength and ferocity of the dragon to fit them in the races. In Chinese tradition, the dragon is a creature of good omen and the symbol of emperors.

Following the on-shore rituals, boatmen paddle the boats out to the sea on a course perpendicular to a temple as the drummer in the prow of each vessel beats out the rhythm. The boats travel to and from the temple three times.

The fervor in which the people perform these ceremonies shows their dedication to the deities. In return, the Gods grant the communities protection from unfriendly sea spirits and bless the villages with happiness and prosperity.

After the races, the head, tail and drum are removed from each boat and stored either in a temple or in a place agreed upon by the community. Incense is burned to propitiate [please] the Gods and the hull of the boats are covered with sand on the shore near a temple or placed on racks and protected with roof-shaped tin foil covers. This ensures the boats will rest until the next Tuen Ng Festival when the whole cycle is repeated."

Crew members prepare to race their elaborately decorated boats during the annual Dragon Boat Festival.

meters, 500 meters, and 250 meters and winners earn victory cups for their efforts; however, most people enter the races for the festive atmosphere and friendly competition.

Made of teak wood, the racing boats sit low in the water like a long canoe and are decorated with an elaborately carved dragon's head at the bow, or front, and a dragon's tail at the stern. Most boats are forty to fifty feet long, and a drummer sits in the front, and beats out the rowing tempo for the twenty to twenty-two rowers sitting shoulder to shoulder from head to stern. Also sitting at the head of the boat is a flag catcher, who will grab the flag floating at the finish line if the boat finishes first; at the tail of the boat is the steerer who controls the boat's direction with a large steering oar.

Mid-Autumn Festival

The third major Chinese festival celebrated in Hong Kong is the Mid-Autumn Festival. Also called the Moon Cake Festival, the Mid-Autumn Festival is celebrated in mid-September. On the night of the festival, families gather to eat special foods and view the full moon, the largest and brightest of the year. Charlie Dittmeier writes, "Families will go to parks and the festival areas and play with their lighted lanterns, traditional ones with candles inside and new ones, in the shape of planes and tanks, with battery-operated lights. They also light dozens of candles and sit around them in the darkness."[84]

Another highlight of the Mid-Autumn celebration is eating moon cakes, also called "re-

A baker makes moon cakes for Hong Kong's autumn Moon Cake Festival.

The Roast Goose King

Kam Shui Fai started his chef career fifty-five years ago cooking roast goose from a street food stall. He soon was able to buy his own restaurant, Yung Kee, since ranked by *Fortune* magazine as one of the top fifteen restaurants in the world. In the article "Hong Kong Food Festival 1997: A Judge's Perspective," food journalist Mietta O'Donnell, describes Kam, who has retired and turned over the family business to his son Kam Kwan Sing, who is himself a master chef.

"[Kam Shui Fai] eventually [bought] four more adjacent buildings [next to his first restaurant at 32 Welling Street, Central, in Hong Kong]. Now the ten story Yung Kee building boasts four levels of restaurants, another of private rooms, offices, a huge kitchen with a massive array of equipment, service kitchens on other levels and on the ground floor, the wonderful entertainment of the open take away [take out] and lunch kitchen. From the street, the geese, chicken and ducks hang in their plump, rich glory. Inside there is frenzied activity as the orders come in for the lunch boxes and also for the diners at the ground floor tables.

Mr Kam . . . was regarded as a legendary chopper, the fastest and most efficient in Hong Kong to dismember and assemble a goose for take away. And, at 85, he is still there every day watching the tables, directing the waiters, filling the teapots and smiling at the ladies. He is a most charming and elegant man, still traditionally dressed in cheung sam [a traditional Chinese one-piece robe]."

union cakes." These cakes are made of a dough wrapped around a paste usually made from walnuts, lotus seeds, dates, egg yolk, fruits, vegetables, meats, and other foods. Dittmeier says that Hong Kong "bakes 25 million of these [moon cakes] . . . made with lard and one or two yolks from either chicken or duck eggs."[85] Boxes of moon cakes are then exchanged as gifts between friends.

There are many different stories related to this holiday, but they all tell how a woman named Chang E became the moon goddess. In one story, Chang E's husband, Hou Ti, saved the earth from burning up from the heat of ten suns by shooting down nine of them with his bow and arrow. The grateful people made him king. Afterward, however, he began abusing his power and killing people. One day he went out to find a magic pill that would give him eternal life. When he returned with the pill, Chang E stole it and swallowed it to save the people from further harm. That night she looked up at the moon and thought to herself how nice it would be to visit it. Quickly, she was swept off into a cloud and her wish was fulfilled, but she could never return to earth.

Hong Kong's Passion for Food

A major part of every festival is the food. For the people of Hong Kong, eating is a passion. As Elizabeth Chin writes in her report on Hong Kong culture, "Food is the centre of life—and leisure—in Hong Kong. Friends and family often get together and chat for hours while eating. It is not uncommon for people to eat out several times a week, and children are often included."[86] With more than nine thousand registered restaurants (and nearly as many unregistered), Hong Kong has more restaurants per person than any city in the world.

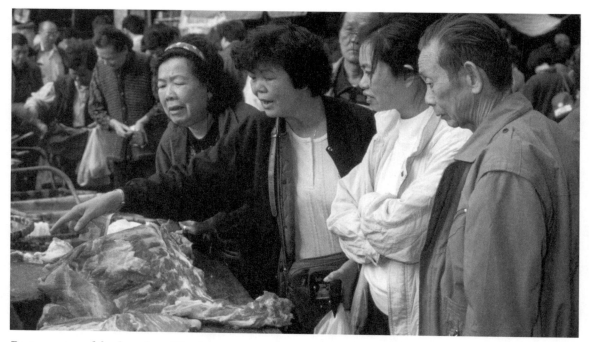

Restaurants and food markets (like this one in Kowloon) are abundant in Hong Kong.

Food is everywhere. On the sidewalks beneath broad umbrellas, cooks toss together quick pancakes, and storefronts display every food imaginable, from fruits and vegetables to chickens, ducks, and other meats hanging from rafters ready for sale.

Some of the most popular places to eat in the city are restaurants called dim sum ("the heart's delight" or "to touch the heart"). Residents associate dim sum with their ancient custom of *yum cha*, or going to tea in the mornings and sitting around talking and eating snacks. Most of the dim sum restaurants are open from early morning to late evening, but they are most popular from midmorning through early afternoon. Each restaurant offers from forty to one hundred different dishes. Some of the favorite snacks include lotus leaves wrapped around fillings such as steamed fried rice, shrimp dumplings, barbecued-pork buns, spicy steamed tripe, and chicken's or duck's feet flavored with black bean and chili sauce. A Hong Kong tourist guide describes dim sum as an

> important social occasion for family gathering on Sunday mornings, for conducting business, meeting friends, or simply to socialize with people. Old people go to teahouses every morning after their Tai Chi exercise; many middle-aged men love to relax themselves with dim sum and tea before a day's work; housewives would often carry their little children for a dim sum brunch to save the trouble of cooking. Dim sum is more than a food category but a special Chinese dining culture, or, to the people who enjoy it daily, an essential part of their life. [87]

The noise and commotion in one of these restaurants is typical of the busy pace of life in Hong Kong, as customers shout to get the attention of waiters who push food carts from table to table.

Eating at dim sum restaurants consumes a lot of time, and in business-centered Hong Kong, people today are often too busy to spend hours in a restaurant eating. They turn to American fast-food restaurants for meals so that they can eat quickly and get back to their work. Domino's Pizza, Pizza Hut, Kentucky Fried Chicken, Jack-in-the-Box, TCBY, and McDonald's are just a few of the dozens of franchises that are popular in the city. In 2001 there were more than 150 McDonald's in Hong Kong, serving an estimated 600,000 customers each day. In fact, according to *Time* magazine, in the late 1990s, Hong Kong was home to "About 25 of the 50 busiest McDonald's restaurants in the world. . . . And the Star House location [at the Star Ferry waterfront landing] in Tsimshatsui [the tip of Kowloon Peninsula] is designated the second-busiest McDonald's on the planet."[88]

Amusement Parks

Another favorite pastime for Hong Kong residents of all ages is visiting amusement parks. Asia's largest theme park, Ocean Park, covers more than two hundred acres on the hilly southern coast of Hong Kong Island. Since its opening in 1977, Ocean Park has hosted more than 52 million people. The most popular attractions at the park are the Atoll Reef, where visitors can observe hundreds of species of fish, and the Shark Aquarium, which contains more

Ocean Park, located on Hong Kong Island, is the largest amusement park in Asia.

than thirty-five species of sharks, including the rare pygmy swellshark. The park also boasts several exciting rides, including the Dragon, Hong Kong's largest roller coaster, and the Abyss ride, an elevator that free-falls 185 feet in a few seconds.

One of Ocean Park's newest attractions is a pair of giant pandas, a gift from mainland China. Because of Hong Kong's hot, humid climate, authorities at Ocean Park had to build a special home for the fourteen-year-old male, An, and twenty-two-year-old female, Jia Jia. The temperature in their new (US) $10.4 million, 1.2-square-mile home is maintained at a constant 68 degrees and the humidity between 50 and 60 percent.

The owners of Ocean Park also operate the Middle Kingdom, a theme park that offers a glimpse of life in ancient China, with replicas of temples, shrines, and pagodas. Street scenes of China's thirteen dynasties are presented by actors in traditional Chinese dress. And in an open-air theater, visitors can watch performances of traditional Chinese acrobats, lion dances, and magic tricks.

The latest attractions in Hong Kong, however, are amusement parks with Western themes. These parks bring in lots of money, both from tourists and locals. Thus, investors continue to build new, Western-themed parks. One such park, Pacific Pier, also located at Ocean Park, offers a small taste of life along the California coast. In addition to exhibits, dining, and shopping, Pacific Pier reproduces the natural habitat of coastal California. And in 2005, Hong Kong will have its own Disney theme park, which the government expects to attract about 1.6 million Hong Kong residents during the first year.

Horse Racing

Hong Kong residents also enjoy a variety of sports, particularly horse racing, which journal-

Hong Kong residents flock to the Happy Valley Racecourse to enjoy horse racing, one of their favorite sports.

ist Paul Moran calls "an obsession in Hong Kong, part of its soul." International Race Day, held in December, "is the biggest sporting event of the year."[89] Between September and June, racing is held twice a week at one of two huge, ultramodern racecourses.

The first of these courses, Happy Valley Racecourse on Hong Kong Island, has a sixty-six-foot-high video screen that displays betting odds and the races. The grounds also include five soccer fields, a jogging path, a roller-hockey rink, and two tennis courts. Although the stands are always packed with more than twenty-five thousand spectators, thousands more watch the races free from their balconies in the high-rise apartments surrounding the tracks.

The second track, located in Sha Tin, opened in 1978. Set beneath towering skyscrapers and along a narrow river, Sha Tin's track has dirt and grass racing surfaces, both of which are considered among the world's best. Irish jockey Michael Kinane, who races in Hong Kong six months a year, says that "Both racecourses are among the best in the world. They lack for nothing. Happy Valley is pretty tight [well made], and you're very aware of the crowd because it's right on top of you. I enjoy it. It gets your heart pumping." [90]

In a typical season, Hong Kong racing fans bet more than US$10 billion. The money goes to the Hong Kong Jockey Club, an organization which operates Hong Kong's racetracks and the city's twice-a-week lottery. Since its beginning in 1884, the Jockey Club has grown into "the single most important element in the structure of business, social life and the regional government," [91] says Moran. It accounts for more than 11 percent of Hong Kong's tax base and funds hospitals and health institutes for Chinese medicine, osteoporosis care, radiotherapy and oncology, and several charities. According to Jockey Club head Larry Wong, "We are . . . Hong Kong's largest private charity donor." [92]

Television

Eating out and going to amusement parks or the racetracks costs a lot of money, money many people in Hong Kong do not have. So, the average resident can be found most evenings at home watching television. At dinnertime, "most Hong Kong people eat and watch the TV Drama [show]," says student May Cheung. "[Television Broadcasts Limited, or TVB,] always draw[s] the public attention because the station employs famous Hong Kong TV stars and singers to play in the dramas. The broadcasting time becomes a part of the daily schedule of many Hong Kong people's lives." [93]

Hong Kong has two free television stations, TVB and ATV (Asia Television Limited), broadcasting in both Cantonese and English with an audience of more than 6.5 million. TVB, however, has by far the largest audience. The station's programming includes a mixture of children's shows, world and local news, financial news and advice, game shows, sports, crime and action dramas, and movies. TVB's English programming includes shows such as *Sesame Street*, the *Wall Street Journal Report*, *NYPD Blue*, *The West Wing*, and *Seinfeld*, as well as movies such as *The Joy Luck Club* and *101 Dalmatians*. Asian football, Hong Kong racing, and other sports are also presented regularly. The second largest broadcasting company, ATV, offers English programs such as the reality show *Survivor* and *The Practice*. Chinese-language programs include soap operas, action and crime shows, historical and romance dramas, variety shows, and general information programs.

Hong Kong also has an independent station financed by the government. Radio and Television Hong Kong (RTHK) produces documentaries and public service programs in addition to dramas, variety shows, and game shows. One Hong Kong college student explains that many of the shows on RTHK are "about real life stories in Hong Kong, like how fraud occurs, real corruption stories, real theft stories, like what's happening in society, our problems." [94]

Music and Movies

Many of the stars the people follow on television also are singing and movie celebrities. The people in Hong Kong listen to every kind of music imaginable. In general, elders tend to favor traditional Chinese and Western classical music. This contrasts sharply with young people's taste for modern, Western-style rock music. By far, though, the most popular music in

Jackie Chan: A Legend

Long before *Rumble in the Bronx* and *Shanghai Noon*, Jackie Chan was popular in Hong Kong (and Asia). He did not start out to be a movie actor, however. Chan's training began at six years old in a Hong Kong Beijing Opera acting school. His study included eighteen-hour days of rigorous and thorough training in music, dance, mime, acrobatics, and martial arts. He made his acting debut when he was eight years old, and until the early 1970s, his roles mostly included stunt acting, performing acrobatic kung fu action scenes in films.

Even after becoming a well-known celebrity, Chan never stopped doing his own stunts. His willingness to perform his own dangerous stunts on the movie set is one of the qualities that has made him a fan favorite to Hong Kong moviegoers. In an interview titled "Jackie Chan," on the *Mr. Showbiz* website, Chan listed the numerous broken bones he suffered from stunts in movies. "My skull, my eyes, my nose three times, my jaw, my shoulder, my chest, two fingers, a knee, everything from the top of my head to the bottom of my feet [has been broken doing movie stunts]."

Chan also gained success by mixing comedy and martial arts. His first starring role came in 1973, but it was not until 1980 that his movies began drawing a mass audience in Hong Kong. Since then, Chan has become not only the most famous Hong Kong film star but also the most popular Asian movie actor in the world. He was awarded an MTV Lifetime Achievement Award in 1995.

Jackie Chan, who began his acting career in Hong Kong, has become the most popular Asian film star in the world.

Hong Kong is Canto-pop (Cantonese pop), a mixture of Western rock or pop sounds and traditional Chinese melodies or rhythms. The fact that the lyrics are written and sung in Cantonese limits the appeal of Canto-pop to Hong Kong and parts of southern China (those are the only regions in which the language is spoken). Furthermore, the Canto-pop stars are eccentric and different, a fact that attracts fans, particularly younger ones. One college student from Hong Kong says that "Everybody [in Hong Kong] listens to canto-pop. . . . What makes this canto-pop culture so popular, why people like it so much is because of how weirdly the singers dress up and how different they try to be. It's more the image, I think, rather than the music itself."[95]

In Hong Kong, tens of thousands of teenagers attend concerts, screaming with excitement for the Canto-pop singers onstage. Fan clubs are widespread and active throughout the city. Among the favorites are Jackie Cheung, Andy Lau, Leon Lai, and Aaron Kwok, referred to as "Canto-Pop's 'Four Heavenly Kings.'"[96] Another favorite is Sam Hui. According to Time magazine, Hui "holds the record for the longest stretch of concerts at the Hong Kong Coliseum—41 performances given during a 37-day period in 1992. Total attendance was 462,481, about 8% of the city's population."[97]

Almost every popular singer in Hong Kong also stars in movies. Andy Lau, one of the "Four Heavenly Kings," was named best actor in 2000 at the nineteenth Hong Kong Film Awards for his movie *Running Out of Time*. Faye Wong, who was once called the "most popular female singer in the Chinese-speaking world,"[98] also is a successful movie actress. And Wong's boyfriend, Canto-pop star Nicholas Tse, became the youngest singer named on Hong Kong's top-ten singer list in 1999; he was only nineteen years old. Since that time he has become a major film star.

Reasons for these crossovers are obvious. Hong Kong residents love movies as much as they love their Canto-pop stars. In fact, although the city is home to only 7 million people, Hong Kong ranks third in the world in film production. Whether going to the theater or renting movies at video stores, Hong Kong residents are avid film fans. Theaters are usually packed. Most people call a couple of days in advance to reserve seats so they do not miss the latest offerings of their favorite celebrities. Today, the most popular movie star is Jackie Chan. One college student says, "People love him. When there is a Jackie Chan blockbuster in the cinemas, it will reach record high levels of revenue earnings."[99]

Mahjong

Whether visiting friends during festivals, gathering to talk in parks, sitting outside high-rises, or relaxing at home listening to music or watching movies, Hong Kong residents enjoy playing mahjong. The loud clicking of ivory or bone rectangular tiles is as familiar as the sounds of shoppers bargaining for goods. According to one website, "Mah Jong is less a game and more a part of the social culture. Passions run high over Mah Jong as do the stakes, and games have been known to run for days."[100]

During a mahjong game, players roll dice and shift tiles around with the handspeed of magicians. The tiles are divided into numbers and suits, similar to a deck of cards. The goal is to get combinations of three or four of a kind. The rules are complicated, and it takes many years of playing to learn the game well. Throughout the game, players gossip loudly, tell jokes, and follow the play of competitors, all at the same time.

The rapid pace of mahjong is just one more example of the fast-paced pressure of life in

Boat passengers enjoy a game of mahjong, a favorite pastime of Hong Kong residents.

Hong Kong. The city's residents manage to adapt their lifestyle, work ethic, and even entertainment to a frenetic, ever-changing society. Such an ability also allows them a broad understanding of the world. On the one hand, they are a people who adhere tightly to their Chinese cultural identity, as is evident from the many festivals they celebrate. On the other, they are a people who embrace new styles of music and films. For these reasons, it is clear that the Hong Kong people are unlike people in most other cities because they share a genuinely international culture.

Notes

Introduction: A Successful Mix of Eastern and Western Cultures

1. Quoted in *Pacific Rim Profiles: Hong Kong*, Asia Pacific Foundation of Canada, 2000. http://collection.nlc-bnc.ca/100/201/300/apfc/profiles/hongkong/HongKong_00-01.pdf.
2. Jan Morris, *Hong Kong*. New York: Random House, 1988, p. 120.
3. Peter Lok, "Hong Kong: Pearl of the Orient," *Meanderings of Thought and Fell*, 1998. www.dragonridge.com/hongkong/hong_kong_action.htm.

Chapter 1: Getting Around

4. Randall van der Woning, *Adventures of a Big White Guy Living in Hong Kong*, "Welcome Home," January 2, 2000. www.vanderwoning.com/three.shtml.
5. Charlie Dittmeier, "Daily Life," August 14, 1998. www.mailing-list.net/cditt/lifeinhk/dailylif98.htm.
6. Dittmeier, "Daily Life," January 5, 1998. http://www.mailing-list.net/cditt/lifeinhk/dailylif98.htm.
7. Dittmeier, "Daily Life," December 4, 1998. http://parish-without-borders.net/cditt/lifeinhk/dailylif98.htm.
8. Quoted in Michael Bociurkiw, "Hong Kong Chokes on Smog: Health, Business, Tourism All Pay Price for Air Pollution," MSNBC, International News, February 22, 2001. http://stacks.msnbc.com/news/530399.asp?cp1=1.
9. Christine Loh, *Clearing the Air—Still a Long Way to Go: A Comprehensive Review of Air Pollution Problems and Solutions*, June 2000. www.citizensparty.org.
10. Morris, *Hong Kong*, pp. 90–91.
11. Morris, *Hong Kong*, p. 166.
12. Phil Parker, "Hong Kong '97—Hong Kong ATC." http://home.netvigator.com/~pashford/parker.html.
13. Maria Cheng, "Up, Up, and Away: After a Rocky Opening, Hong Kong's Chek Lap Kok Has Established Itself as Asia's Best Airport," *Asiaweek*, August 18, 2000. www.asiaweek.com/asiaweek/features/asiabest2000/life.airport.html.

Chapter 2: City Life

14. Morris, *Hong Kong*, pp. 63, 67.
15. Wayan Vota, "Vertical Living in Hong Kong," November 8, 2000. http://wayan.net/journal/china/nov_8.htm.
16. Morris, *Hong Kong*, p. 27.
17. Lee Foster, "Hong Kong: Citizens in a Bamboo Cage." www.fostertravel.com/HONGKO.html.
18. Andy Carvin, "Hong Kong Reunion," 1999–2000. http://edweb.gsn.org/seasia/hongkong1.html.
19. Keith B. Richburg, "Change of No Consequence," *Washington Post*, April 29, 1997. http://washingtonpost.com/wp-srv/inatl/longterm/hongkong/nochange.htm.
20. Keith B. Richburg, "Amid the Affluence, City's Homeless Are Nearly Invisible," *Washington Post*, March 30, 1997. http://washingtonpost.com/wp-srv/inatl/longterm/hongkong/homeless.htm.
21. Jeff Booth, "Perspectives: Hong Kong, China," *Student World Traveler Magazine*, November 1999. www.studenttraveler.com/mag/11-99/hong.cfm.
22. David Clarke, "Seasonal Festivals in Hong Kong: Diary of Clarke (June 18,

1997)," *Hong Kong 1997: Lives in Transition.* www.pbs.org/pov/hongkong/diaries/Clarke/6-18-97.shtml.

23. Quoted in Paul Murphy, "Crime Around the World," *World & I,* June 1, 1999.

Chapter 3: Family and Home Life

24. Quoted in Murphy, "Crime Around the World."

25. Elizabeth Chin, "Hong Kong: A Cultural Profile," Catholic Immigration Centre, 1993. http://cwr.utoronto.ca/cultural/english2/HongKong/hongkongENG.htm#_1_6.

26. Quoted in Edward A. Gargan, "Four Faces of Hong Kong: Daily Life in Heady Times. The Tycoon: With Pride and Emotion in Past and Future, Business as Usual," *New York Times,* June 19, 1997. www.nytimes.com/specials/hongkong/061997hk-expect-tycoon.html.

27. Gargan, "Four Faces of Hong Kong. The Tycoon."

28. Peter Lok, "Hong Kong Again." www.dragonridge.com/hongkong/hong_kong_again.htm.

29. Dittmeier, "Daily Life," May 12, 1998. www.mailing-list.net/cditt/lifeinhk/dailylif98.htm.

30. Dittmeier, "Daily Life," December 25, 1997. www.mailing-list.net/cditt/chinahk/sub-hk9698.htm.

31. Zainab Aziz et al., "The Penthouse in Hong Kong." www.uzone21.com/WOK/english/features/penthouse_eng/index.html.

32. "Being Squeezed by the Competition? Pressured Shoppers Grab Convenience, ACNielsen Research Reveals What's Hot in Supermarkets," ACNielsen Hong Kong, September 28, 2000. http://dmd2523s24.mozart.2day.com/news.cfm?NewsID=136.

33. Anthony Fung, "Formal vs. Informal Use of Television and Sex-Role Stereotyping in Hong Kong (Statistical Data Included)," *Sex Roles: A Journal of Research,* January 2000. www.findarticles.com/m2294/2000_Jan/63016016/p1/article.jhtml.

34. Quoted in Yulanda Chung, "A Wealth of Problems: Growing Poverty Has Become a Time Bomb," *Asiaweek,* November 10, 2000. www.cnn.com/ASIANOW/asiaweek/magazine/2000/1110/nat.hk.html.

35. Quoted in Murphy, "Crime Around the World."

36. Hong Kong Federation of Youth Groups (HKFYG), "The Views of Youth on Marriage," Youth Opinion Polls No. 81, August 31, 2000. www.hkfyg.org.hk/yrc/english/yr-polls-81-e.html.

Chapter 4: Education

37. Marcia Hohmann, "Morning Ritual Provides a Rare Moment of Peace," *SCMP,* February 24, 2001. http://special.scmp.com/Educ...ltext_asp_ArticleID-20010223155738948.asp.

38. Quoted in Murphy, "Crime Around the World."

39. HKFYG, "Young People's Outlook on Life," Youth Opinion Polls No. 41, July 1997. www.hkfyg.org.hk/yrc/english/yr-polls-41-e.html.

40. Ruth Hayhoe, "The Future of Education in Hong Kong," *HKDF Newsletter,* December 1998. www.hkdf.org/newsletters/9812/1298_3.htm.

41. HKFYG, "Students' Views on Examinations," Youth Opinion Polls No. 43, June 1997. www.hkfyg.org.hk/yrc/english/yr-polls-43.html.

42. HKFYG, "Do Aims of Revising the Educational System a [sic] Matter to Young Students?" Youth Opinion Polls No. 63, March 5, 1999. www.hkfyg.org.hk/yrc/english/yr-polls-63-e.html.

43. Tsui Hon-Kwong, "Put an End to Dreaded Dictation," *SCMP,* January 20, 2001. http://special.scpm.com/Template/PrintArticle.asp.

44. Hon-Kwong, "Put an End to Dreaded Dictation."

45. Quoted in Katherine Forestier, "Search for Brave, New School System," *Class mateAsia.com,* March 1999. www.classmateasia.com/news_content.php3?TITLE_ID=F199903WHA.

46. Quoted in Katherine Forestier, "Battle over Reform of Secondary School Selection," *ClassmateAsia.com,* January 2000. www.classmateasia.com/news_content.php3?TITLE_ID=F200001CHA.

47. Anna Wu Hung-yuk, "Equalising Opportunities in Hong Kong—What Needs to Be Done?" *HKDF Newsletter,* June 2000. www.hkdf.org/newsletters/0006/0006_5.htm.

48. Quoted in Carrie Lee, "Moving Mania for Top Schools in Hong Kong," *Independent,* July 28, 2000.

49. Quoted in Lee, "Moving Mania for Top Schools in Hong Kong."

50. Quoted in Peter Cordingley, "Wired for Life," *Asiaweek,* May 12, 2000. www.asiaweek.com/asiaweek/magazine/2000/0512/cover1.html.

51. Quoted in Todd Crowell, "Tongues Clack over Speaking Chinese in Hong Kong Schools," *Christian Science Monitor,* January 14, 1998.

Chapter 5: Religion

52. Dittmeier, "Daily Life," December 10, 1999. www.mailing-list.net/cditt/lifeinhk/dailylif99.htm.

53. Morris, *Hong Kong,* p. 125.

54. Dittmeier, "Daily Life," April 6, 1998. www.mailing-list.net/cditt/lifeinhk/dailylif98.htm.

55. Morris, *Hong Kong,* pp. 125–26.

56. Morris, *Hong Kong,* pp. 121–22.

57. Lok, "Hong Kong: Pearl of the Orient."

58. Morris, *Hong Kong,* p. 122.

59. Lok, "Hong Kong: Pearl of the Orient."

60. Quoted in "Making Sense of Feng Shui: Insights in the East," August 20, 1999. www.bbc.co.uk/makingsense/fengshui/east.shtml.

61. *Passport Hong Kong, the Work Environment.* June 30, 1996. http://elibrary.com/s/edumark/getdoc.cgi?id=0~0&dinst=.

62. Howard G. Chua-Eoan, "World: Ideas How to Keep the Dragons Happy: The Chinese Art of Feng Shui Can Ensure a Prosperous Building," *Time,* June 22, 1987.

63. Glenda Winders, "Feng Shui Practiced, Not Preached; Hong Kong Wary of Being Called Superstitious," *Washington Times,* February 3, 2001, p. E3.

64. Dittmeier, "Daily Life," June 30, 1999, www.mailing-list.net/cditt/lifeinhk/dailylif99.htm.

65. Van der Woning, "Welcome Home."

Chapter 6: Earning a Living

66. Quoted in Rick Browne and James Marshall, eds., *Hong Kong: Here Be Dragons.* New York: Stewart, Tabori & Chang, 1992, p. 176.

67. Quoted in Rahul Jacob, "The Uplifting Saga of Asia Inc.," *Time Asia,* Golden Anniversary Issue, 1996. www.time.com/time/asia50/b_5.html.

68. Chin, "Hong Kong: A Cultural Profile."

69. Rahul Jacob, "From Father to Son: One Company's Dilemma," *Time,* Hong Kong 1997: Special Issue. www.time.com/time/hongkong/special/contents.html.

70. Frank Welsh, *A Borrowed Place: The History of Hong Kong.* New York: Kodansha International, 1993, p. 461.

71. Gargan, "Four Faces of Hong Kong: Daily Life in Heady Times. The Fishmonger: A Lifetime of Staying Afloat and Dodging the Sharks." www.nytimes.com/specials/hong kong/061997hk-expect-fish.html.

72. Quoted in Gargan, "Four Faces of Hong Kong: Daily Life in Heady Times. The Waiter: Reading the Tea Leaves for a Fresh Season of Life." www.nytimes.com/specials/hongkong/061997hk-expect-waiter.html.

73. Linda To, "Hong Kong Women Workers," Hong Kong Women Workers Association, Hong Kong Country Report, *Dignity in Labor,* July 23, 2000. www.itcilo.it/english/actrav/telearn/global/ilo/frame/epzhong.htm.

74. William Keng Mun Lee, "Industrial Dualism, Income, and Gender Inequality in Hong Kong," *Asian Affairs: An American Review,* March 22, 1997.

75. Citizens Party, "Families." www.citizens party.org/community/families.html.

76. Susan Berfield, "Why Women Stay Single," *Asiaweek,* June 27, 1997. www.asiaweek.com/asiaweek/97/0627/cs1.html.

77. Quoted in Joanne Lee-Young, "Friends, Family, and Funding," *Industry Standard,* November 13, 2000. www.thestandard.com/article/display/0,1151,20034,00.html.

78. Michael Klosson, "'Rule of Law, Openness' Make Hong Kong What It Is," October 26, 1999, speech to the American Chamber of Commerce, Hong Kong, U.S. Department of State, *International Information Programs, the United States and China, Speeches.* http://usinfo.state.gov/regional/ea/uschina/klosson.htm.

79. Sunny Kai-sun Kwong, "Hong Kong Facing New Challenges—Three Years After the Handover," *CSIS,* Spring 2000. www.csis.org/html/HKUpdateSpr-00.PDF.

80. Chung, "A Wealth of Problems."

Chapter 7: Enjoying Life

81. Hong Kong Tourist Association, "Kung Hei Fat Choy!" November 14, 2000. www.hkta.org/canada/pr/pr20001114c.html.

82. Randall van der Woning, *Adventures of a Big White Guy Living in Hong Kong,* "The Year of the Dragon: Kung Hei Fat Choy!" February 12, 2000, www.vander woning.com/thirtythree.shtml.

83. Van der Woning, "The Year of the Dragon."

84. Dittmeier, "Daily Life," October 5, 1998. www.mailing-list.net/cditt/lifeinhk/daily lif99.htm.

85. Dittmeier, "Daily Life," October 6, 1998. www.mailing-list.net/cditt/lifeinhk/daily lif99.htm.

86. Chin, "Hong Kong: A Cultural Profile."

87. YPTOURIST.com, "Features: Dim Sum." http://yptourist.com/dine_feature/dimsum 2.htm.

88. "Lifestyle: 97 Reasons to Love Hong Kong," *Time,* Hong Kong 1997: Special Issue. www.time.com/time/hongkong/special/best.html.

89. Paul Moran, "Racing Utopia: Playing the Horses in Hong Kong in Public Service and Obsession," *Newsday,* February 25, 2001.

90. Quoted in Ed McNamara, "Horse Racing Finds a Home in Hong Kong," *ESPN.com,* January 9, 2001. www.espn.go.com/horse/s/1999/1215/234798.html.

91. Moran, "Racing Utopia."

92. Quoted in Moran, "Racing Utopia."

93. May Cheung, "May's Media Profile," February 7, 2001. www.discovery.mala.bc.ca/web/cheungy/mp.htm.

94. Menka, "Interview with Tutuwa," *Book of Culture.* Red Cross Nordic United World College, 2001. http://w3.rc-nuwc.uwc.org/webpages/GlobalConcerns/CULTURE/bookofculture/Menka.htm.

95. Menka, "Interview with Tutuwa."

96. Graham Earnshaw, "Hong Kong Cultural Icons Fad on Chinese Mainland," Hong Kong Handover: Culture, 1997. www.nando.net/newsroom/nt/621CHIzzz.html.

97. "Lifestyle: 97 Reasons to Love Hong Kong."

98. Quoted in Anthony Spaeth, "The Arts/Music: She Did It Her Way: Canto-Pop Princess Faye Wong Broadens Her Appeal with a Quirkier Sound," *Time International,* October 14, 1996.

99. Menka, "Interview with Tutuwa."

100. "Hong Kong and Macau," Waiviata International. www.waiviata.com.au/HongKong/HkgGen/hkcultur/hkcultur.htm.

For Further Reading

Books

Rick Browne and James Marshall, eds., *Hong Kong: Here Be Dragons*. New York: Stewart, Tabori & Chang, 1992. An excellent photographic introduction to life in Hong Kong. The accompanying discussion of Hong Kong is also good but dated.

Robert Green, *China*. San Diego: Lucent Books, 1999. A look at China's evolution from a rural country to a dynastic culture to a modern nation. Includes information on Hong Kong.

Jan Morris, *Hong Kong*. New York: Random House, 1988. This is a thorough and lively discussion of Hong Kong's history, including short profiles of various influential people up to 1988. Morris has an intimate knowledge of the Hong Kong lifestyle.

Internet Sources

"Asia's Best for the Year 2000," *Asiaweek*. www.asiaweek.com/asiaweek/features/asiabest2000/index.html.

Edward A. Gargan, "Four Faces of Hong Kong: Daily Life in Heady Times," *New York Times*, June 19, 1997. www.nytimes.com/specials/hongkong/061997hk-expect.html.

Hong Kong Federation of Youth Groups, Youth Opinion Polls. www.hkfyg.org.hk/yrc/english/yr-polls.html.

Hong Kong Tourism Association, "Interactive Stories: Legend of the Dragon." www.hkta.org/gallery/interactive.html.

Public Broadcasting System, *Hong Kong '97: Lives in Transition*, May 31, 2001. www.pbs.org/pov/hongkong.

Time, Hong Kong 1997: Special Issue, 1997. www.time.com/time/hongkong/special/contents.html.

Works Consulted

Books

China: 7000 Years of Discovery. China's Ancient Technology. Beijing: China Books & Periodicals, 1983. An outstanding source for a survey of Chinese contributions to science and technology. Includes chapters on such fields as the discovery of paper, printing, gunpowder, silk, Chinese astronomy, medicine, mechanics, bronze sculpture, and architechture. Plenty of illustrations.

Frank Welsh, *A Borrowed Place: The History of Hong Kong.* New York: Kodansha International, 1993. An excellent, detailed history of Hong Kong, but more on the level for college classes.

Periodicals

Howard G. Chua-Eoan, "World: Ideas How to Keep the Dragons Happy: The Chinese Art of Feng Shui Can Ensure a Prosperous Building," *Time,* June 22, 1987.

Todd Crowell, "Tongues Clack over Speaking Chinese in Hong Kong Schools," *Christian Science Monitor,* January 14, 1998.

"Four-Fifths of HK Workforce Covered by Retirement Schemes," Xinhua [China News Agency], December 7, 2000.

Carrie Lee, "Moving Mania for Top Schools in Hong Kong," *Independent,* July 28, 2000.

William Keng Mun Lee, "Industrial Dualism, Income, and Gender Inequality in Hong Kong," *Asian Affairs: An American Review,* March 22, 1997.

Paul Moran, "Racing Utopia: Playing the Horses in Hong Kong in Public Service and Obsession," *Newsday,* February 25, 2001.

Paul Murphy, "Crime Around the World," *World & I,* June 1, 1999.

Anthony Spaeth, "The Arts/Music: She Did It Her Way: Canto-Pop Princess Faye Wong Broadens Her Appeal with a Quirkier Sound," *Time International,* October 14, 1996.

Glenda Winders, "Feng Shui Practiced, Not Preached; Hong Kong Wary of Being Called Superstitious," *Washington Times,* February 3, 2001.

Internet Sources

Zainab Aziz et al., "The Penthouse in Hong Kong." www.uzone21.com/WOK/english/features/penthouse_eng/index.html.

"Being Squeezed by the Competition? Pressured Shoppers Grab Convenience, ACNielsen Research Reveals What's Hot in Supermarkets," ACNielsen Hong Kong, September 28, 2000. http://dmd2523s24.mozart.2day.com/news.cfm?NewsID=136.

Susan Berfield, "Why Women Stay Single," *Asiaweek,* June 27, 1997. www.asiaweek.com/asiaweek/97/0627/cs1.html.

Better Hong Kong Foundation, "Advancements in the Quality of Life." www.bhkf.org/modsoc/html/qol.html.

Michael Bociurkiw, "Hong Kong Chokes on Smog: Health, Business, Tourism All Pay Price for Air Pollution," MSNBC, International News, February 22, 2001. http://stacks.msnbc.com/news/530399.asp?cp1=1.

Jeff Booth, "Perspectives: Hong Kong, China," *Student World Traveler Magazine,* November 1999. www.studenttraveler.com/mag/11-99/hong.cfm.

"The Bottom Line Ranked by Net Users Per 10,000 Population," *Asiaweek*, March 23, 2001. www.asiaweek.com/asiaweek/magazine/2001/0323/bottomline.html.

Roderic Broadhurst, "Crime Trends in Hong Kong," 2000. www.hku.hk/crime/rb-crime trends.htm.

Andy Carvin, "Hong Kong Reunion," 1999–2000. http://edweb.gsn.org/seasia/hongkong1.html.

Jasmine Brion Chatman-Hamlett, "The World Gone MAD with Over-Consumption," *Odyssey*. World Trek for Service and Education, July 8, 2000. www.worldtrek.org/odyssey/asia/071200/071200jashkmad.html.

Maria Cheng, "Up, Up, and Away: After a Rocky Opening, Hong Kong's Chek Lap Kok Has Established Itself as Asia's Best Airport," *Asiaweek*, August 18, 2000. www.asiaweek.com/asiaweek/features/asiabest2000/life.airport.html.

Angelica Cheung, "Cultural Revolution: With a Pre-1997 Influx of High-Flying Immigrants from China, the 'Melting Pot' of Hong Kong's Chinese Society Is Again in Ferment," *Asiaweek*, June 28, 1996. www.asiaweek/96/0628/feat1.html.

May Cheung, "May's Media Profile," February 7, 2001. www.discovery.mala.bc.ca/web/cheungy/mp.htm.

Cheung Chi-fai, "Buddhist Monks to Pacify Post 'Ghosts,'" *SCMP*, March 17, 2001. http://hongkong.scmp.com/ZZZQMANJDKC.html.

Elizabeth Chin, "Hong Kong: A Cultural Profile," Catholic Immigration Centre, 1993. http://cwr.utoronto.ca/cultural/english2/HongKong/hongkongENG.htm#_1_6.

Chinese Cuisine Training Institute. www.vtc.edu.hk/~ccti/eng/all.htm.

Chinese University of Hong Kong, "CUHK's Faculty of Medicine Joins Hong Kong Marathon" [press release], February 19, 2000. www.cuhk.edu.hk/ipro/000219e.htm.

Yulanda Chung, "A Wealth of Problems: Growing Poverty Has Become a Time Bomb," *Asiaweek*, November 10, 2000. www.cnn.com/ASIANOW/asiaweek/magazine/2000/1110/nat.hk.html.

Citizens Party, "Action Plan for Gender Equality," policy paper, program for 1998–2000, April 1998. www.citizensparty.org/community/eo/womenpp1.html.

———, "Families." www.citizensparty.org/community/families.html.

David Clarke, "Seasonal Festivals in Hong Kong: Diary of Clarke (June 18, 1997)," *Hong Kong 1997: Lives in Transition*. www.pbs.org/pov/hongkong/diaries/Clarke/6-18-97.shtml.

Peter Cordingley, "Wired for Life," *Asiaweek*, May 12, 2000. www.asiaweek.com/asiaweek/magazine/2000/0512/cover1.html.

Toni Dabbs, "Wong Tai Sin Temple: Worth a Fortune," *Travel Lady*, March 3, 1999. www.travellady.com/articles/article-wong-tai.html.

Charlie Dittmeier, "Daily Life," 1998. http://parish-without-borders.net/cditt/lifeinhk/dailylif98.htm.

———, "Daily Life," 1996–1998. www.mailing-list.net/cditt/chinahk/sub-hk9698.htm.

———, "Daily Life," 1998. www.mailing-list.net/cditt/lifeinhk/dailylif98.htm.

———, "Daily Life," 1999. www.mailing-list.net/cditt/lifeinhk/dailylif99.htm.

Dragon Boat Association of Edmonton [Canada], "The History of Dragon Boat Racing," 1999. www.agt.net/dragon/history01.html.

Graham Earnshaw, "Hong Kong Cultural Icons Fad on Chinese Mainland," Hong Kong Handover: Culture, 1997. www.nando.net/newsroom/nt/621CHIzzz.html.

Ethelbert, "Save Our Students: Diary of Ethelbert (June 9, 1997)," *Hong Kong 1997: Lives in Transition.* www.pbs.org/pov/hongkong/diaries/Ethelbert/6-9-97.shtml.

Seth Faison, "After a Night of Parties, Nothing Feels Different," *New York Times,* July 1, 1997. www.nytimes.com/specials/hongkong/070197hongkong-scene.html.

Katherine Forestier, "Battle over Reform of Secondary School Selection," *Classmate Asia.com,* January 2000. www.classmateasia.com/news_content.php3?TITLE_ID=F200001/CHA.

———, "Search for Brave, New School System," *ClassmateAsia.com,* March 1999. www.classmateasia.com/news_content.php3?TITLE_ID=F199903WHA.

Lee Foster, "Hong Kong: Citizens in a Bamboo Cage." www.fostertravel.com/HONGKO.html.

Anthony Fung, "Formal vs. Informal Use of Television and Sex-Role Stereotyping in Hong Kong (Statistical Data Included)," *Sex Roles: A Journal of Research,* January 2000. www.findarticles.com/m2294/2000_Jan/63016016/p1/article.jhtml.

Ruth Hayhoe, "The Future of Education in Hong Kong," *HKDF Newsletter,* December 1998. www.hkdf.org/newsletters/9812/1298_3.htm.

"HK Blames Rave Parties for Rise in Juvenile Crime," *Muzi.com,* January 18, 2001. http://news.muzi.com/ll/english/1040437.shtml.

Marcia Hohmann, "Morning Ritual Provides a Rare Moment of Peace," *SCMP,* February 24, 2001. http://special.scmp.com/Educ...ltext_asp_ArticleID-20010223155738948.asp.

———, "Ten Significant Trends Among Youth," *Youth Trends in Hong Kong 2000.* www.hkfyg.org.hk/yrc/english/yr-hkyt-00-e.html.

"Hong Kong and Macau," Waiviata International. http://www.waiviata.com.au/HongKong/HkgGen/hkcultur/hkcultur.htm.

Hong Kong Tourist Association, "Kung Hei Fat Choy!" November 14, 2000. www.hkta.org/canada/pr/pr20001114c.html.

———, "Tops for Transportation," Hong Kong Superlatives, May 9, 2000, p. 2. www.hkta.org/superlatives/transport2.html.

Tsui Hon-Kwong, "Put an End to Dreaded Dictation," *SCMP,* January 20, 2001. http://special.scpm.com/Template/PrintArticle.asp.

Anna Wu Hung-yuk, "Equalising Opportunities in Hong Kong—What Needs to Be Done?" *HKDF Newsletter,* June 2000. www.hkdf.org/newsletters/0006/0006_5.htm.

"Hungry Ghosts Festival: Gui Jie, the Mid-Year Festival," *Chinese Festivals,* Federation of Chinese Canadians in Scarborough [Ontario], February 26, 2001. www.interlog.com/~fccs/hungry.htm.

"Jackie Chan," *Mr. Showbiz,* 2000. mrshowbiz.go.com/celebrities/people/jackiechan/bio.html.

Rahul Jacob, "From Father to Son: One Company's Dilemma," *Time,* Hong Kong 1997: Special Issue. www.time.com/time/hongkong/special/contents.html.

———, "The Uplifting Saga of Asia Inc.," *Time Asia,* Golden Anniversary Issue, 1996. www.time.com/time/asia50/b_5.html.

Michael Klosson, "'Rule of Law, Openness' Make Hong Kong What It Is," October 26, 1999, speech to the American Chamber of Commerce, Hong Kong, U.S. Department of State, *International Information Programs, the United States and China, Speeches.* http://usinfo.state.gov/regional/ea/uschina/klosson.htm.

Sunny Kai-sun Kwong, "Hong Kong Facing New Challenges—Three Years After the Handover," *CSIS,* Spring 2000. www.csis.org/html/HKUpdateSpr-00.PDF.

Niki Law, "Ghost-Ridding Ceremony Performed at Post," *SCMP*, March 20, 2001. http://hongkong.scmp.com/ZZZCWMNJDKC.html.

Joanne Lee-Young, "Friends, Family, and Funding," *Industry Standard*, November 13, 2000. www.thestandard.com/article/display/0,1151,20034,00.html.

Peggy Leung and Dan Woodley, "Asia's Best for the Year 2000: The Best Transport," *Asiaweek*. www.asiaweek.com/asiaweek/features/asiabest2000/env.park.tran_sb1.html.

"Lifestyle: 97 Reasons to Love Hong Kong," *Time*, Hong Kong 1997: Special Issue. www.time.com/time/hongkong/special/best.html.

Christine Loh, *Clearing the Air—Still a Long Way to Go: A Comprehensive Review of Air Pollution Problems and Solutions*, June 2000. www.citizensparty.org.

Peter Lok, "Hong Kong Again." www.dragonridge.com/hongkong/hong_kong_again.htm.

———, "Hong Kong: Pearl of the Orient," *Meanderings of Thought and Fell*, 1998. www.dragonridge.com/hongkong/hong_kong_action.htm.

"Making Sense of Feng Shui: Insights in the East," August 20, 1999. www.bbc.co.uk/makingsense/fengshui/east.shtml.

"The Manufacturing Sector," *Hong Kong Annual Report 1999*. http://info.gov.hk/hkar99/eng/06/06/_03_content.htm.

Ed McNamara, "Horse Racing Finds a Home in Hong Kong," *ESPN.com*, January 9, 2001. www.espn.go.com/horse/s/1999/1215/234798.html.

Menka, "Interview with Tutuwa," *Book of Culture*. Red Cross Nordic United World College, 2001. http://w3.rcnuwc.uwc.org/webpages/GlobalConcerns/CULTURE/bookofculture/Menka.htm.

Mietta O'Donnell, "Hong Kong Food Festival 1997: A Judge's Perspective," 1997. www.miettas.com/travel/hongkong.html.

Pacific Rim Profiles: Hong Kong, Asia Pacific Foundation of Canada, 2000. http://collection.nlc-bnc.ca/100/201/300/apfc/profiles/hongkong/HongKong_00-01.pdf.

Passport Hong Kong, the Work Environment. June 30, 1996. http://elibrary.com/s/edumark/getdoc.cgi?id=0~0&dinst=.

Phil Parker, "Hong Kong '97—Hong Kong ATC." http://home.netvigator.com/~pashford/parker.html.

"Public Urged to Help Prevent Hillfires During Ching Ming," March 24, 2001. www.info.gov.hk/gia/general/200103/24/0323251.htm.

Keith B. Richburg, "Amid the Affluence, City's Homeless Are Nearly Invisible," *Washington Post*, March 30, 1997. http://washingtonpost.com/wp-srv/inatl/longterm/hongkong/homeless.htm.

———, "Change of No Consequence," *Washington Post*, April 29, 1997. http://washingtonpost.com/wp-srv/inatl/longterm/hongkong/nochange.htm.

Michele Tang, "Gender Inequality in Household," *Varsity*, May 1999. www.jlm.cuhk.edu.hk/varsity/9905/inequ.htm.

Linda To, "Hong Kong Women Workers," Hong Kong Women Workers Association, Hong Kong Country Report, *Dignity in Labor*, July 23, 2000. www.itcilo.it/english/actrav/telearn/global/ilo/frame/epzhong.htm.

Robert Tompkins, "Hong Kong's Chinatown," *Hong Kong Duet—Voices of Old Hong Kong*, January 1, 1999. www.thingsasian.com/goto_article/article.835.html.

Wayan Vota, "Vertical Living in Hong Kong," November 8, 2000. http://wayan.net/journal/china/nov_8.htm.

Randall van der Woning, *Adventures of a Big White Guy Living in Hong Kong*, "Welcome

Home," January 2, 2000. www. vanderwoning. com/twentynine.shtml.

———, *Adventures of a Big White Guy Living in Hong Kong,* "The Year of the Dragon: Kung Hei Fat Choy!" February 12, 2000, www.vanderwoning.com/thirtythree.shtml.

———, *Adventures of a Big White Guy Living in Hong Kong,* "Yep, Transportation Is What It's All About," November 1998. www.vanderwoning.com/three.shtml.

"Youths Link Happiness with Money," *SCMP,* September 11, 2000. http://business.scmp.com/Search/SearchArticles.idq.

YPTOURIST.com, "Features: Dim Sum." http://yptourist.com/dine_feature/dimsum 2.htm.

Index

Picture Credits

Cover photo: © Tony Stone Images
© AFP/CORBIS, 26
AP Photo, 55
© Josef Beck/FPG International, 61
© Bettmann/CORBIS, 66
© Bohemian Nomad Picturemakers/CORBIS, 37
Ace or Adrian Bradshaw/Archive Photos, 11
© Rick Browne/Photo Researchers, Inc., 68
© CORBIS, 15
© Macduff Everton/CORBIS, 63
© Michael Freeman/CORBIS, 34
© Georg Gerster/Photo Researchers, Inc., 48
© Sylvain Grandadam/Photo Researchers, Inc., 23
© Andres Hernandez/Getty Images, 72
© Alex Hofford/Getty Images, 76
© Jack Hollingsworth/CORBIS, 40
© Wolfgang Kaehler/CORBIS, 81
© Reed Kaestner/CORBIS, 13, 27, 29
© Kelly-Mooney Photography/CORBIS, 82, 86

© Earl & Nazima Kowall/CORBIS, 62, 78
© Bob Krist/CORBIS, 25
© Harvey Lloyd/FPG International, 9
© James Marshall/CORBIS, 77
© Ron McMillan/Liaison/Getty Images, 42, 44
© Michel Porro/Getty Images, 18, 21
Reuters/Larry Chan/Archive Photos, 39, 65
Reuters/Claro Cortes IV/Archive Photos, 38
© Reuters NewMedia Inc./CORBIS, 84
Reuters/Bobby Yip/Archive Photos, 35, 70, 75
© Paul A. Souders/CORBIS, 45
© Keren Su/FPG International, 31
© Telegraph Colour Library/FPG International, 58
© Travel Ink/CORBIS, 43, 47, 53, 80
© David & Peter Turnley/CORBIS, 50
© Nik Wheeler/CORBIS, 17
© Alison Wright/CORBIS, 57

About the Author

Tony Zurlo taught in Nigeria with the Peace Corps and at a teacher's university in China. He lives in Arlington, Texas, with his wife, an artist/educator from China. His publications include the books *Japan: Superpower of the Pacific* and *China: The Dragon Awakes*. His poetry, fiction, reviews, and essays have appeared in over sixty literary magazines and newspapers.